∧ Top Notes

Tracy Chevalier's
Girl with a Pearl Earring

Study notes for VCE English

Justine Clarke

A
FIVE SENSES
PUBLICATION

Always for Shannen, my girl with cat earrings and Paul who knows everything I don't know.

Five Senses Education Pty Ltd
2/195 Prospect Highway
Seven Hills 2147
New South Wales
Australia

Clarke, Justine
Top Notes –Girl with a Pearl Earring
ISBN 1- 74130 –303 – 6

TOP NOTES VCE ENGLISH SERIES

This series has been created to assist VCE students of English in their understanding of set texts set for the text response section of their paper. Top Notes are easy to read, providing analysis of issues and discussion of important ideas contained in the texts.

Particular care has been taken to ensure that students are able to examine each text in the context of the VCE. These notes should assist you to be able to clearly understand the texts set for study.

Each text includes:

- Plot summary
- Character analysis
- Setting
- Thematic concerns
- Language studies
- Essay questions and a modelled response
- Study practice questions
- Useful quotes

I am sure you will find these Top Notes useful in your studies of VCE English.

Bruce Pattinson
Series Editor

CONTENTS

STUDYING A FICTION TEXT

The medium of any text is very important. If a text is a novel this must not be forgotten. Novels are *read*. This means you should refer to the "reader" but the "responder" can also be used when you are referring to the audience of the text.

The marker will want to know you are aware of the text as a novel and that you have considered its effect as a written text.

Remembering a fiction text is a written text also means when you are exploring *how* the composer represents his/her ideas you MUST discuss language techniques. This applies to any response you do using a novel, irrespective of the form the response is required to be in.

Language techniques are all the devices the author uses to represent his or her ideas. They are the elements of a fiction that are manipulated by authors to make any novel represent its ideas effectively! You might also see them referred to as stylistic devices or narrative techniques.

Every fiction uses language techniques differently. Some authors have their own favourite techniques that they are known for. Others use a variety to make their text achieve its purpose.

Some common language techniques are shown on the diagram that follows.

LANGUAGE TECHNIQUES

Setting – *where does the action take place? Why? Does the setting have symbolic meaning?*

Main Character portrayal/development: *How does the character develop?* **What is the reader to learn from this?**

Minor Character use: *How does the author use the minor characters to represent ideas about themes or major characters?*

Narrative Person: *what is the effect this has on the narrative and the reader's response to it?*

LANGUAGE TECHNIQUES

Humour

Symbols and motifs: *how is repetition of image/idea used to maximise the novel's effect?*

Images: *similes, metaphors, personification,*

Dialogue: *not just what is said but how is important to idea representation*

Tone: *not just of character comments but also of the narration*

Conflict: *the action, Man vs man, Man vs nature, and/or Man vs himself*

Aural techniques: *Alliteration, assonance and onomatopoeia, rhythm*

THE AUTHOR

Tracy Chevalier grew up in Washington DC. Moving to England in 1984 she worked as a reference book editor. In 1994 she graduated from The University of East Anglia with a Master of Arts in Creative Writing. She is married and has one son.

Chevalier says that the inspiration for *Girl with a Pearl Earring* came when she was lying in bed one morning considering ideas for her next novel. She had a poster of the painting hanging in her room having always admired Vermeer's paintings. It suddenly occurred to her that a story lay behind the look on the girl's face.

"I wonder what Vermeer did to her to make her look like that. Now there's a story worth writing."

Chevalier recognised the atmosphere, mystery and conflict present in much of Vermeer's work, especially in the women depicted, and wanted to tell the story of at least one of these women.

Chevalier has won numerous awards for her many novels, some of which include, *Falling Angels, The Virgin Blue* and *The Lady and the Unicorn.* She is recognised for her attention to detail, finely drawn characters and superb evocation of place and atmosphere.

Girl with a Pearl Earring has recently been made into a feature film starring Colin Firth as Vermeer and Scarlett Johanssen as Griet.

The painting itself hangs in The Royal Cabinet of Paintings, Mauritshuis, The Hague.

CONTEXT

Chevalier has stated in interviews that she has created this novel out of a desire to come up with the story behind one of Johannes Vermeer's most famous paintings. While the author's context is important in any work, the more significant context here is the painting itself and the life of its creator, Vermeer.

The historical context of Vermeer and his work is not just the backdrop for this story of a young girl's sexual awakening, but is in fact the foundation on which the imagined story is built. Chevalier's fascination with Vermeer is one shared with many art lovers since the rediscovery of his work in the mid 19th Century. Vermeer became popular again due to the influence of the Impressionists, who believed, as Vermeer did, that colour was a function of the response to light in a painting. His actual use of a camera obscura allowed him to reproduce reality as he saw it, not necessarily as it was, another popular idea with Impressionists. Art critics believe that Vermeer's settings were symbolic, designed to represent something about the subject of the painting. In the same way, Chevalier uses Vermeer's paintings in a symbolic manner to represent aspects of society, characters and ideas. She has conducted thorough research into a number of Vermeer's paintings and uses them as subtext for her narrative. A working knowledge of the following paintings will help you to understand more clearly some of the settings, issues and characters in the novel.

*View of Delft
*Woman with a Pearl Necklace
*The Concert
*Woman with a Water Pitcher

*The Milkmaid
*The Girl with the Wineglass
*A Lady Writing
*Girl with a Pearl Earring.

Delft itself was a society in which an individual was restrained by the prevailing social paradigms. These restrictions were based on religion, gender, class or financial status.

Delft in Vermeer's time was known for its breweries, tile industry and tapestries, but during a time of economic decline, the city experienced a rise in artistic expression, its most famous exponent being Johannes Vermeer. Delft may have attracted artists because of its reputation for cleanliness and quiet. It is no surprise that Griet and her mother are obsessively clean, as housewives in Delft were known for fanatical cleanliness. Delft Society was mainly Protestant, a stronghold of conservative Calvinism but Dutch society in general was said to be quite tolerant of religious difference as can be seen in Griet's father's attitude towards Catholics.

The Guild of St Luke's main function was to limit the number of outside artists selling within Delft and taking away business from the locals. It also organised apprenticeships for young artists and artisans and attempted to look after members affected by misfortune. Vermeer himself was admitted to the Guild in 1653 and later was elected headman, proving he was highly respected by his fellow artists. The Guild became the centre of his social life, as Delft offered little else in the way of entertainment.

Vermeer is not recognised by art critics as an innovator in his technique. However, he is noted for his precision and attention to detail and his use of innovative ideas in a city that was known for its artistic output. Art critic Albert Blankett says of Vermeer,

"His great achievement lies instead in the recognition of new possibilities within the existing forms and in his ability to recast them in original ways."

Vermeer was married to Catharina Bolnes in April 1653. She was much younger than he was and her mother, Maria Thins, needed to be convinced of Vermeer's artistic and financial worth before she would allow her daughter to marry him.

They did have a large family, Catharina giving birth to fourteen children of whom eleven survived.

It is also true that Vermeer produced a relatively small amount of paintings in his life due to his meticulous nature. Other details from Chevalier's book exist contextually also. It is true for example that Catharina did settle a debt to the family baker with a painting after Vermeer's death, to the value of 617 guilders.

The differences in religion in this society also predominate and provide conflict for Chevalier to work with. Griet's Protestant background conflicts sharply with the Catholicism of the Vermeer's. Vermeer himself was a Calvinist who converted to Catholicism in order to convince his prospective mother-in-law that he was a good enough match for her daughter.

Context is important when studying a text as knowledge of the background of the text will help you to9 write an informed response, however be selective in what you choose to include. Your own context will affect what you see in the text also.

"It's not the painting that is Catholic or Protestant...but the people who look at it and what they expect to see."

PLOT OUTLINE

Griet is told she is to work for the Vermeers.

Griet learns that her main duty is to clean Vermeer's studio.

Her father gives her a tile as a parting gift.

Griet arrives at the Vermeer's and meets the children.

Griet slaps Cornelia, making an enemy.

Griet meets Pieter the butcher and his father.

Griet settles into her new life and routine

Griet connects with Vermeer

Griet looks through the camera obscura.

Griet shuns Agnes while at the market.

Griet is not allowed to visit her family

Pieter tells Griet about The Plague.

Griet visits Frans to tell him about Agnes.

Van Ruijven notices Griet.

The Quarantine is lifted but Agnes is dead.

Franciscus's birth
feast preparations

Van Ruijven corners
Griet at the birth feast
and tells Vermeer he
should paint her.

Griet begins assisting
Vermeer in the studio

Cornelia breaks Griet's
tile.

Vermeer teaches
Griet about colours
and their bond grows

Pieter courts Griet

Vermeer admits to
learning from Griet

Griet is accused of
stealing a comb and
Vermeer takes her
side against his family

Vermeer begins to
paint Griet

Van Leeuwenhoek
warns Griet to be

Griet's relationship
with Pieter advances
but she wants Vermeer

Vermeer sees Griet's
hair, she has sex
with Pieter

Vermeer orders Griet
to pierce her own ears so
she can wear the earrings.

Pieter proposes to Griet
Vermeer touches her
face

Catharina sees the
finished painting. Griet
leaves the Vermeers

Griet marries
Pieter
and has two sons.

Vermeer dies, and Griet
is summoned to the
house and
given the pearl earrings.

Griet pawns the
earrings
paying Vermeer's debt

PLOT SUMMARY

Pages 3 - 6

The novel opens with the main character Griet's surprise that her mother has not informed her that they are to receive visitors. The first person narrative immediately emphasises Griet's perspective and the reader feels her disquiet at the unexpected intrusion despite her apparent calm.

She is chopping vegetables and while she does so, she listens to the voices in the next room making distinctions between the other characters based on what she can hear in their voices. The female visitor sounds as, "bright as polished brass" and the man's voice is "low and dark like the wood I was working on", immediately establishing a connection between Griet and the male visitor. Through Griet's description, it is clear that wealth can be heard and it is an uncommon sound in her home.

While Griet is obviously aware of her status, she is proud and does not want the visitors to think badly of her.

"I was glad that earlier I had scrubbed the front step so hard."

Her mother's voice is described as "a cooking pot, a flagon," underlining her working class status and her practical nature. Already, a conflict between classes is established. Griet carefully prepares herself to greet the visitors, cleaning her hands on her apron and pressing her lips together to smooth them.

An incompatibility between the visiting couple (at least in the eyes of Griet) is obvious in their heights. The woman is taller than her husband is but this does not mean she has an advantage, as he obviously has the power to control and silence her. Griet compares her own family to this couple, realising that they are all small including her brother and father. She is referring to stature but status is also obvious.

The woman, whom we soon learn is Catharina Vermeer, is there to inspect Griet and assess her suitability as a maid for her household. Ironically, she is under close scrutiny herself from Griet. Catharina is pregnant and nervy. Vermeer needs to calm her when the knife drops to the floor and Griet notes that he speaks, "as if he held cinnamon in his mouth."

Griet lets her perfectionist nature show when she corrects the arrangement of the vegetable wheel she has been making and Vermeer notices. He speaks directly to her, questioning her about the vegetable wheel and is intrigued by her sensitivity to colour.

"The colours fight when they are side by side, Sir."

Vermeer purposely drops a vegetable into the wrong place, testing her resolve but she fights the impulse to correct it, recognising his intention. This is the first of many times that he tests her.

The interaction between them does not go unnoticed by Catharina whose annoyance with her husband is directed at Griet. The conflict and upcoming contest between the two women is immediately evident.

After the Vermeers leave, Griet's mother explains what is to happen. Griet is to become the Vermeer's maid and work for them for eight stuivers a day, returning home only on Sundays to visit her family. The implication is made that Griet has no choice in this matter as her father has lost his trade due to an accident that has left him blind and the family needs the money in order to survive. Griet is shocked to learn that the family she is to live with and work for are Catholic, establishing another important contrast. They live on the Oude Langendijk where it intersects with the Molenpoort and Griet recognises this place as Papist's Corner. The reality that even the neighbours will be Catholic is jarring to her.

As Griet watches her mother scoop the precisely arranged vegetables into the soup, the reader realises that it is not only the carefully laid out vegetable wheel that is ruined for Griet but also any hopes she had for the future.

Q. Outline the conflict situations that are established in this opening section.

Pages 6 – 8

Griet climbs the stairs to visit her father. He sits close to the window hoping to at least see light and shade.

Through the first person narrative, Griet explains how her father, a tile painter, lost both his sight and his livelihood after the kiln he was working with exploded in his face. His eyes have been sown shut and the irony and pathos of this scene is obvious, as this man who was so sensitive to colour and art is unable to see anything.

He has heard the discussion downstairs and obviously feels guilt and regret that Griet is forced to go into service. He attempts to reassure his daughter by explaining that her new master is a good man and will treat her fairly. The omission of any mention of his wife is an ominous sign however.

The close relationship between Griet and her father is clear as they discuss a painting they saw together. It was a view of Delft, where they live, and they both remember the smallest details of the artwork. Griet's father explains that the artist is Johannes Vermeer and that this is the man she has met and will be working for. She has been employed specifically to clean his studio.

Q. Describe the relationship between Griet and her father.

Pages 8 - 9

Griet and her mother make preparations for her to leave. She is given a spare cap, collar and apron so that she will always have a clean set. Both mother and daughter have a strong sense of pride in their appearance and do not wish to appear slovenly.

Griet's mother gives her a tortoiseshell comb that belonged to her grandmother. This becomes very important to Griet, as not only is it a treasured possession; it reminds her of home. She also packs a prayer book for the times when she feels she needs to escape Catholicism. Her mother then explains to Griet that it is a direct result of her father's accident that this position became available. Vermeer is the headman of the Guild of St. Luke that her father belongs to and the Guild "looks after its own". Lack of choice and the family's pride are once again obvious as her mother explains that the insurance money they received after her father's accident did not go far and "we won't take public charity".

Griet's mother says that part of her job will be to clean without 'moving anything'. Griet is puzzled at how to do this but realises that her father's blindness has ironically prepared her for this position. Because he is blind and relies on knowing where things are, she has had to clean objects and then place them back carefully where her father remembers them to be. However, she is daunted by the prospect of doing this for a great artist who is a stranger to her.

Q. How has the position at the Vermeer's become available?

Pages 9 – 10

Her ten-year-old sister, Agnes, is upset at Griet's departure as she has already had to say goodbye to her brother when he left for his apprenticeship at age thirteen. The lack of choice the children have is emphasised by Frans's situation. He hates the apprenticeship but cannot leave due to his father's sacrifice in saving up the fee. Once again the sad irony is conveyed as the plan had been for Frans to return and start up a family business with his father, but the accident has put an end to those hopes. Frans is resentful of the position he has been placed in and as a consequence, rarely visits home. This further distresses Griet's father who feels responsible for his family's misfortune.

"Now our father sat by the window and never spoke of the future."

Q. Explain Griet's comment about her father's apprenticeship making him what he is today.

Pages 10 – 24

On the day that Griet leaves, her father gives her a tile that is special to her. It was one he painted when he still had his sight and depicts a boy and girl who were obviously inspired by his two eldest children. Griet notes that, "the girl wore her cap as I wore mine" and then describes how she wears her cap and how it allows her to hide her face (and emotions) at will.
Griet leaves and as she walks through the streets of Delft, images of the hardworking lifestyle of the working class are depicted. Griet considers how her little sister's life will change now that she will have to take on all of Griet's chores, leaving little time to just be a child and play.

Griet is also aware of people's eyes on her as she walks. She acknowledges that she will become the topic of gossip, however does not anticipate any unkindness to her family. The people of this society are aware of the precarious position they are all in and misfortune could visit any of them just as it has to Griet's family.

As she walks through Market Square, noise and movement is conveyed and the busy and repetitive lives of the working class will provide a sharp contrast with the quiet severity of the Vermeer's home.

The walk acts as a stimulus for Griet to reminisce about her childhood and the simplicity of the games she played with her brother and sister. In one particular game, the three siblings would throw stones into the canal imagining what lay at the bottom of the dark shadows in the water. Griet admits she was fearful of the game and the canal will become symbolic of her fears later.

In the centre of The Square she stands on the eight-pointed star that is cut into the ground, remembering another game that her siblings would play. She recalls that she had thought of the star as both the centre of the town as well as the centre of her life. She has followed all points of the star except for the one that leads to Papist's Corner and as she turns to go there now she realises her life is no longer simple and that she is entering an almost foreign world.

"I knew no Catholics."

Griet displays an obvious distrust of Catholics although she notes that they were tolerated in Delft as long as they did not flaunt their religion. The tolerance of her father is mentioned as he has told her that Catholics are no different to anyone else.

When she reaches the house the five Vermeer children are outside. They are in age order; Maertge, Cornelia, Lisbeth,

Aleydis and Johannes. The two eldest go to announce her arrival and the youngest tell Griet about their grandmother, Maria Thins, who owns the house.

Griet compares the house to her own and is glad that it is not as grand as she had expected it to be, hinting that she feels intimidated by whom she is working for.

The maid Tanneke comes out to meet her and is immediately suspicious and unwelcoming. Griet cannot help comparing herself to Tanneke and notes that her apron was "not as clean as mine."

Tanneke's body language shows Griet that she is threatened by her arrival. She recognises the potential for bullying and carefully considers an appropriate response that will not invoke Tanneke's anger.

As she follows Tanneke into the house she realises she is entering not just a new house, but also a new world and a new life.

"I stepped across the threshold."

The first thing she notices inside are the many paintings on the walls, but she later discovers that Vermeer has painted none of them. The painter supplemented his income by trading and selling paintings and rarely kept his own works in the house, as he needed to sell them.

Griet feels very uncomfortable when she sees a large painting of the crucifixion in one room and is similarly disturbed by a number of graphic portrayals of biblical scenes.

She is introduced to the formidable Maria Thins, Catharina's mother, and is then taken on a tour of the house, through the kitchens, storeroom, laundry and courtyard. She is shown her sleeping place, which is a small room underneath one of the storerooms, only accessible by climbing down a ladder. Dropping her bundle into the room, she is reminded of the monsters her brother and sister believed were at the bottom of the canal and her trepidation is evident.

In the Vermeer's bedroom she sees nineteen more paintings and those with religious connotations obviously bother Griet as she sees it as a sin to depict or represent biblical events.

Tanneke points out the studio that Griet will be cleaning and then makes a point of showing her "my mistress's rooms" (Maria Thins) as a clear confirmation of who is more important in the household. It is obvious to Griet that Tanneke feels she has competition.

Griet's main duties include the laundry, going to the meat hall and fish stalls, and cleaning Vermeer's studio. She is also to help Tanneke with food preparation and any other errand that Catharina requires. She is answerable to Catharina.

Griet cleverly asks Tanneke how she has managed to do all the household chores alone, in an attempt to get on the older maid's good side and it seems to work. She also accepts that as she is new and young, all the difficult tasks will be hers.

Later, Griet is challenged by Cornelia and responds by slapping her on the face. Her instinctive decision wins the respect of the other girls but she makes an instant enemy of cunning Cornelia. Griet's intuition tells her that Catharina will have the same attitude to her as Cornelia does and this frightens her a little as she knows she cannot slap her mistress into submission. Her inferiority is further brought home to her as Cornelia throws a pot in the canal in an act of revenge and Griet must find a way to retrieve it. She does so with the help of a man in a boat who teases her about getting a kiss as payment. She avoids his advances and effectively deals with Cornelia by threatening to tell Maria Thins.

She is suddenly struck by the belief that Vermeer has been watching the whole scene from the upper window; however she does not actually see him.

Q. Why is Griet so disturbed by the paintings she sees in the Vermeer's home?

Pages 24 – 29

For the first time in her new home, Griet sees Catharina and is struck by how proud the woman is of carrying her large set of keys. Griet thinks they look uncomfortable but Catharina obviously sees them as a status symbol. They represent how many rooms are in her house and therefore are an indication of what she controls.

Griet's descriptions of Catharina are never complimentary, her resentment is obvious. In their first interaction Griet realises that she doesn't actually know how to be a maid. She speaks to Catharina and immediately can tell by her reaction that her mistress is annoyed with her. However she is also aware that Catharina needs to learn how to be a mistress, having had no servant of her own before. She actually has little power in the house, as she must submit to the wishes of both her husband and mother and even Tanneke does not really answer to her. Apart from her children, Griet is the only one she can bully without interference.

Griet decides to help her "without seeming to."

Afterwards, Griet is surprised by the family's ability to just sit and be content together. This is one of the only pleasant images of Catharina teaching her girls to sew and laughing at her baby's antics.

Tanneke takes Griet to the market and Maertge accompanies them. The meat market is described as busy with its thirty-two butchers all competing for customers who squabble and barter for the freshest meat. The reader becomes aware of the poverty of Griet's family as she smiles at the butcher "we used to buy our meat from before my father's accident."

She is happy to see a familiar face and be in a familiar place but she is then introduced to the Vermeer's family butcher, Pieter and is not impressed by "his blood-spattered apron."

She feels threatened and disconcerted by so many new experiences and people in one day especially as she is alone and not supported by the security of her own family. Because she is in a strange environment that she does not wish to be in, she begins to find fault with everything new and cannot help comparing her new life to her old life. She even compares the butchers, noting that,

"Our butcher always wore a clean apron when he was selling, changing it whenever he got blood on it."

The butcher places the chops and tongue that Griet purchases into her meat pail and then Tanneke introduces Griet to the fishmonger, as she is to alternate meat and fish each day. When they return to the house, Griet is overwhelmed by a desire to go home and hand her mother the chops as,

"We had not eaten meat in months."

Q. Assess Griet's attitude towards Catharina. Do you think she is completely fair to her?

Pages 29 – 32

Griet eats with Tanneke after helping prepare the meal and she is glad to be able to eat what the family eats. She also notices the better quality of the food. She then describes the rest of her day, which will become her routine for every day except Sunday.

Griet's morning is spent doing laundry; washing, hanging out and later ironing all of the family's clothes. After fetching the meat or fish, she helps clean up and she and Tanneke mop the floors of the kitchens and storerooms. Her afternoons consist mainly of ironing.

Tanneke mentions to Griet that Catharina will spend most of the last weeks of her pregnancy in bed. Tanneke's disdain for Catharina is obvious.

Griet sees Vermeer going to dinner but he does not acknowledge her. Griet refers to Vermeer as 'he'.

She eats dinner with the girls in the crucifixion room, while the adults eat tongue in the dining hall. Afterwards she feels Maria Thins watching her as she irons.

Vermeer has a male guest after dinner, a plump man with a long feather in his hat.

Griet notes that although the work is no harder than it was at home, she is more exhausted as she does not have the relief of being able to laugh or talk to anyone.

She climbs down to the cellar to spend her first night alone. Despite the claustrophobic description of the space, Griet does not seem frightened of anything except the painting that hangs at the end of her bed. The painting is of Christ on the cross and it disturbs her because of the intense emotion evident on both Christ's and Mary Magdalene's faces. The pain is vividly portrayed and even though she cannot see the painting after blowing out her candle, the image is imprinted in her mind and she cannot sleep.

Q. Why does Griet sleep so badly on her first night at the Vermeer's?

Pages 32 – 39

The next morning in the light, Griet is able to study her sleeping space and attempts to make it more comfortable. She notices some still life paintings in the room leaning against the wall and is tempted to replace the crucifixion scene with one of them. The children have already told her, however, that they sometimes play in that room, and she knows Cornelia would use the information against her if she could. Later, Griet decides to cover the painting with her apron and is able to sleep much more soundly as a result. The painting reminds her of her Protestantism and she wonders how the rest of the household views her.

"I had never before been outnumbered."

Catharina takes Griet to the studio for the first time and Griet makes an immediate connection between her father and the room. It smells of linseed oil, like her father used to when he returned from the factory each day and this smell allows her to feel comfortable in at least one room of her new environment.
In contrast, Catharina is obviously uncomfortable in her husband's studio. She stands in the doorway as Griet goes in to investigate further. This is another step in the unspoken rivalry between Griet and Catharina. They have been distrustful of each other from the outset and now Griet wants her to leave the only comfort zone she has been able to find.

"She made me nervous, waiting in the doorway for me to make a mistake."

Griet is reminded not to move anything in the area that is being painted. When Catharina hears Johannes cry she leaves, giving Griet the privacy she so desires. She opens

Top Notes

the window and looks out, spying Tanneke scrubbing the step. Tanneke does not notice Griet but a cat walking by, does. The cat makes Griet feel uncomfortable, as if she is being watched and she subsequently connects Cornelia with having catlike qualities.

Griet sees herself in the mirror and is surprised at her own reflection. She is anxious and feeling guilty but she also notices her own beauty in her glowing skin. This is a sign of her burgeoning sexuality.

As she moves around the studio she looks for any sign of home especially a tile painted by her father amongst the ones that line the walls, but there are none. Everything is new and strange.

She notices that the room is quite large but not cluttered with furniture as Vermeer has only what he needs to paint. The room feels different to the rest of the house because it is,

"...empty of the clutter of everyday life."

She realises that this is a place where Vermeer can shut himself away from his wife, his children and his servants. The quietness is emphasised. The whitewashed and pale grey room is itself a blank canvas in which the painter can create works of great beauty.

Griet begins to clean but shows her awareness of the importance of light by not cleaning the dirty windows. The cleaning becomes a complex puzzle for Griet to solve. The objects she must clean under are difficult to rearrange exactly as they were especially items like a blue cloth and a letter.

The next section is an elaborate description of the intricate process of moving the letter.

"I laid my fingers against the edges and drew in my breath, then removed the letter, dusted and replaced it all in one quick movement."

Constantly anxious about getting this job right, Griet is also aware that she is being tested and that only 'he' would know if something was not correctly replaced. She measures the space between each item carefully with her hand, using her tactile sense and the same shrewd judgement that she uses to sum up people.

"I measured each thing in relation to the objects around it and the space between them."

She does not know what to do about the cloth so she leaves it. Carefully avoiding the painting, which she is afraid to view, she cleans the rest of the studio, but is eventually caught staring at the painting by Maria Thins. The old woman does not rebuke her, and in fact tells her about the painting; that it is of Van Ruijven's wife and that Vermeer has managed to make her look beautiful even though she is not.

Griet refers to a painting growing, showing that she considers them a living entity and then admits that she always remembered this one because it was the first one of Vermeer's that she was to see.

The conversation with Maria Thins allows the older woman to see intelligence in Griet. They discuss the painting and then contemplate it together. The painting provokes an interesting reaction in Griet who feels she needs to know the creator of this work and then realises that studying something beautiful so closely makes it lose something. This will later have great relevance to her own life.

As she leaves, Maria Thins is still studying the painting.

Q. What do you learn about Maria Thins from her interaction with Griet in this section?

Pages 39 – 42

Griet feels the tension between herself and Tanneke who is at this point aligned with Cornelia (doing her hair). While she makes a lot of comments about Tanneke's incompetence to the reader, Griet is wary of openly confronting her. To be difficult, she tells Griet to visit the butchers instead of the fishmonger and Griet realises that it is because she is jealous of the fact that Griet is allowed into the studio when no one else is except for Maria Thins. Tanneke childishly announces that Vermeer once painted her and that,

"Everyone said it was his best painting"

Griet takes this opportunity to flatter her into a better mood, saying how much she would like to see the painting herself and then reminding Tanneke that Van Ruijven, who bought the painting, probably looks at it every day. Having successfully pacified Tanneke, Griet escapes to the markets alone, refusing the girls requests to accompany her. This offers her a brief respite from the strangeness of her new life.

At the meat market, Griet says hello to her old family butcher and the conversation allows Griet to vocalise her despair. She tells the butcher,

"I have no choice I'm afraid."

This statement actually refers to the Vermeer's choice of butcher but it also applies to the situation Griet finds herself in. The butcher brings up the new butcher's handsome son, also named Pieter but Griet is dismissive of this new information.

When Griet moves along to the new butchers she refuses to "give him the compliment he craved." A pattern that she continues with both father and son throughout the novel. When she first sees Pieter the son, she recognises how handsome he is and her description of him is ambiguous as she sees his eyes resting on her as if they are, "a butterfly on a flower." This image seems romantic at first with its connotations of gentleness and appreciation of beauty but there is also the implication of a creature that is sucking out and devouring the sweetness from an innocent blossom.

Griet blushes despite herself.

Another test ensues for Griet as Pieter's father attempts to sell her a leg of mutton that is not fresh. She immediately recognises the deliberate error and haughtily refuses the joint. Her decision is watched closely by both Pieters and they offer her a better quality joint. She is disturbed to see the glance that passes between father and son as she understands the implications for her future and once again feels that she has little control over her own life.

Q. Why does Griet adopt a haughty tone with Pieter the butcher and his son?

Pages 42 – 43

Back at the Vermeer's, Catharina tells Griet that her husband is satisfied with the cleaning but she refuses to look at Griet herself. Once again Griet is aware that she has passed her test and will now be able to stay. It hits her that this is her life now.

What follows is a description of Griet's daily life and the duties she is expected to fulfill.

"The rest of the day passed much as the first had, and as the days to follow would."

She must clean the studio, visit the meat or fish stalls, and complete a three-day cycle of laundry. She also helps with the preparation and serving of the family meals, watches the children and mops the floors at night.
She is still disturbed by the crucifixion painting at the end of her bed so she begins to cover it with her apron.

Q. Why does Griet feel the need to wash an apron every day?

Pages 43 – 46

When Catharina takes Griet to the studio the next day, Griet asks about the windows and whether she should clean them. Catharina does not "see" what she means and Griet must explain the importance of light to a painting. The fact that she doesn't understand shows her incompatibility (in Griet's eyes) for Vermeer.
Catharina is flustered and is forced to ask her husband about the light. Griet notices that she refuses to look at the painting or come into the studio. When she returns, Griet is proved right and the windows are to be left. This is another round in the competition between them.
Griet notes that nothing very obvious changes from day to day in the painting studio but she can 'feel' that Vermeer has been there. She doesn't see the man himself for several days but remarks on hearing his voice.

"Hearing his voice made me feel as if I were walking along the edge of a canal and unsure of my steps."

Griet has already noted that she feels a connection to the canal but is afraid of what lies at its depths and the same could be said for the way she feels about Vermeer.

Often when she thinks about him she remembers their first interaction and how he noticed her obsession with the vegetable colours.

When she finally runs into him, she is very aware of their difference in status and cannot meet his eyes. As for Vermeer, he has not started to look at Griet in any capacity at this point.

"He neither smiled nor did not smile at me."

Griet sees Van Ruijven and his wife for the first time in person. She describes Van Ruijven as a fake personality who likes to give out false compliments and is ostentatious in his dress and mannerisms.

Later when his wife speaks to Griet about where to leave Catharina's pearls, Griet is unable to separate the real woman from the image in the painting. Another reminder of status is given here as Van Ruijven's wife refuses to leave the pearls in Griet's keeping and Griet accepts (grudgingly) that maids cannot be trusted.

Q. Why is Griet so fascinated when she meets Van Ruijven's wife?

Pages 46 – 47

Small details in this section create a vivid picture as Griet describes her Saturday with the girls. Later, Catharina, Tanneke, Maria Thins and Maertge go to the market and Griet is left with the younger children. Griet is disappointed not to go as she has been hoping desperately to run into her mother and sister.

Cornelia is acting quite sweetly and Griet begins to feels that she has misjudged the little girl. However, even though there are hints that Cornelia is warming to Griet, she rightly feels that the girl cannot be trusted.

While she is holding the baby in the courtyard, Vermeer appears and Griet feels a very strong reaction to him that she must hide behind the baby. He also hides his expression behind his hat as opposed to Catharina who is an open book.

His children ask to go with him on his errand but he refuses and Griet again notes that he has not spoken to her since the vegetable question in her own home.

Q. Where is Vermeer going on his errand?

Pages 47 – 51

On Sunday Griet is ready to go home and visit her family but is stopped on the way by Maria Thins who informs her that Catharina is not well and will be in bed for a few days. Griet attempts to flatter Maria Thins but the old woman sees through her flattery. She appreciates Griet's cleverness, however, perhaps tired of the ignorance of both Tanneke and her own daughter.

Griet goes home and is surprised at how many differences she notices between her mother's home and the Vermeers. Probably nothing has actually altered but because her life has changed so much she is projecting this onto the landscape around her.

Agnes is especially excited to see her big sister at home and she fires questions at Griet. Griet feels comfortable and is proud to hand over her small wage to help her family. Her father feels her hands and his guilt can be seen in his statement.

"Already you have the scars of hard work."

Griet makes light of her work in an attempt to relieve his guilt and her mother offers a practical solution to keep her hands soft. Once again there is a distinct difference in class as Griet's mother offers homemade remedies while the Vermeers can afford the apothecary.

Griet describes her new life in an interesting way. Her explanation to the reader tells only what she has left out of the story for her family. This shows both her love and concern for her loved ones but also her capacity to lie and tell others what she thinks they want to hear.

Griet's mother's pride is obvious as she refuses the offer of free meat that the family butcher has offered to Griet. Griet finds she relaxing as she spends more time with her family and when she attends church with them she is comforted by the familiarity of the people and the service.

"I felt my back relaxing into the pew and my face softening from the mask I had worn all week."

Later, her father questions her about Vermeer and she is able to state honestly that she has seen very little of him. At his urging, she describes the painting and her affinity with her father can be seen in her description of the light, so that he understands her, despite his disability.

"The light on the back wall is so warm that looking at it feels the way the sun feels on your face."

Her father is able to ascertain easily that cleaning the studio is the only happy part of her day but she does not confirm this for him despite agreeing in her own mind. While eating the simple dinner that her mother has lovingly prepared, Griet realises sadly that she has already grown accustomed to the trappings of her new life and is subconsciously comparing the two situations.

"I loved it because I knew it, but I was aware now of its dullness."

After farewelling her parents, Agnes accompanies Griet to Market Square and admits how lonely she is without her big sister. Griet promises to visit every Sunday and arranges to meet her sometimes in the market but she is conscious of only speaking to Agnes if she is alone.

Q. What is Griet's mother's solution for her daughter's work hardened hands?

Pages 51 – 56

Griet begins to feel more comfortable in her new position even though she occasionally has problems with Catharina, Cornelia and Tanneke. She suspects that Maria Thins is her advocate and the others bow in deference to the matriarch, therefore following her lead where Griet is concerned. Griet wonders about Maria Thins' reasons for liking Griet and then acknowledges the improvements she has made since arriving. The meat is better, the laundry is up to date and most importantly, the painter is happier with his clean studio and therefore should become more productive. She assumes this last point as she has no way of knowing how Vermeer feels about the job she is doing. Griet is wise enough to know that she should not take credit for better housekeeping and to keep on Tanneke's good side she deflects any compliments on to the older maid.

Griet admits to avoiding Catharina as much as possible assuming her mistress dislikes her. Griet is increasingly negative in her descriptions of Catharina.

It is obvious that Griet openly dislikes her mistress calling her ungainly and virtually mocking the idea that Catharina sees herself as the graceful lady of the house. Griet shows her disrespect in a number of ways and while she feels her place as far as Vermeer and Maria Thins are concerned, she obviously sees Catharina as more of a rival than a superior.

In response to Griet's question about why there are not more maids to share the workload, Tanneke informs her that the Vermeers can barely afford to pay Griet. Because Vermeer takes so long to paint a portrait, the family has to wait a long time before they get income and it is later made clear that they are very dependant on the patronage of Van Ruijven. Griet is surprised that Catharina owns so many expensive things when the family will have to scrape to pay for a wet nurse for the new baby.

Tanneke has informed Griet that Catharina always likes to employ a wet nurse, as she believes feeding her own child will lessen her chances of having a large family.

Griet is also told that Vermeer only paints two or three paintings per year which is enough to keep them comfortable but not make them rich. Griet realises that this is part of his perfectionist nature, that he will not sacrifice the quality of his artistic expression for money. Catharina's wish that he paint more shows her ignorance of the intricacy of his work.

Maria Thins is very aware of Catharina's unfairness to the servants but does not interfere with the way her daughter treats others. So while Griet knows that Maria Thins likes her, she cannot depend on her to defend her against anyone else in the house. Griet also notes that Tanneke is not very good at her work and recognises that this is what makes her so defensive.

The studio becomes an escape for Griet just as it has for Vermeer. By this stage she has experimented and discovered a way to effectively clean the dark blue cloth. She sees that nothing seems to change in the room, neither the setting nor the painting itself. But eventually small changes become obvious to her. Her relationship with Vermeer builds up like this as small details start to accumulate. He does something, she notices.

Cornelia continues to be a problem for Griet because of her unpredictability. She admits that she has become very fond of the girls but still does not trust Cornelia. The insidious nature of the little girl is conveyed as it is obvious she is watching Griet closely and looking for an opportunity for revenge. On one occasion Griet is tempted to touch the Catharina's satin mantle until she sees Cornelia watching her and smiling slyly.

Q. What advice does Tanneke give Griet about how to handle Catharina?

Pages 56 – 57

Griet allows Maertge to accompany her to the market one morning. They are watching a kite being flown and Griet is smiling at Maertge's enjoyment when she notices her sister watching Maertge enviously, obviously seeing her as a replacement. Griet is conscious of the fact that she has avoided talking about the girl's ages, especially Maertge's, as she has not wanted to make Agnes jealous. She discreetly signals for Agnes to stay away afraid of what she could do.

Griet feels dreadful because she knows she has hurt Agnes but resolves to explain the situation to her on Sunday. She is ashamed as she turns her back on her confused and hurt sister.

Q. Why has Griet neglected to tell Agnes about Maertge?

Pages 57 – 64

Catharina asks for Griet's help while Griet is doing the laundry in the courtyard. She insists on knowing where Vermeer and his visitor are and when Griet assures her that they are in the studio, she asks for assistance to get up. She is by now heavily pregnant and Griet describes her as moving,

"...down the hallway like a ship with its sails full."

Tanneke explains to Griet that Catharina is hiding from van Leeuwenhoek; the acquaintance of Vermeer's who lends him a special box to help him with his painting. The reason Catharina is afraid of this man is because she broke his special box and has now been banned from entering the studio.

The box becomes the catalyst for a change in the relationship between Vermeer and Griet. It is described as,

"a wooden box about the size of a chest for storing clothes in. A smaller box was attached to one side, with a round object protruding from the side of it."

Griet does not touch the box when she first sees it in the studio, but is very curious and looks at it quite closely while she works. When she has finished cleaning she studies the box very closely, crossing her arms and forming a barrier against the thing she does not understand. She senses Vermeer's presence in the room and he asks her if she would like to look in the box. He tries to explain what it is but she is confused.

Vermeer calls the box a camera obscura and then demonstrates how it is used. He removes his coat and hat and using the cloak as a cover over his head, he looks into the box. Griet feels uncomfortable when he removes his cloak but she is really disturbed when he offers to let her look into the box covered by his cloak while he stands and watches her.

Despite knowing how bad it would look if someone walked in on them, Griet feels she has no choice but to do as he asks and therefore agrees to look in the box covered by the cloak that was just around her master's head. She feels drunk.

"I felt as if I had drunk my evening beer too quickly."

However, her confusion and fear escalates when she opens her eyes and sees the image from the painting in the box. He patiently answers her many questions, pleased at her interest and she notes that he looks directly at her for the first time.

"Something changed in his face as if he had been looking over my shoulder but was now looking at me."

She realises it is rare for him to talk to anybody who understands or is interested in his work, at least artistically, as opposed to Maria Thins and Catharina's truly mercenary interest. It is obvious that Griet wants Vermeer to respect her intelligence.

"More than anything I wanted him to think I could follow what he said."

However, he comments only on her wide eyes and she blushes at his attention. She asks to be left alone to study the painting through the camera obscura and he agrees with amusement.

When he is gone she scrutinises the image closely and describes it almost as if it is a photograph. This is very strange to her, as she has only ever seen paintings before, however once she grows used to it, she is fascinated by the image.

Vermeer returns and questions her. He explains that the camera obscura is a tool "to help him see." Because his eyes "do not always see everything."

He gets carried away explaining how the tool works before suddenly realising the inappropriateness of this discussion with a maid. Griet is left feeling as if she has been tricked again.

Q. Draw the camera obscura from the description given.

Pages 64 – 68

Alone later that night, Griet considers the interaction and begins to understand how Vermeer can see things differently. The next day when she returns to the studio, the camera obscura is gone and the map has been removed from the painting and the scene and Griet understands why.

She notes however that the sudden change "upsets" her. This shows that she has started to feel as if she has an understanding with the painter and is disturbed if he does something she does not anticipate.

When she visits the meat hall, Pieter the son is there alone. He obviously likes her as he flirts with her but has difficulty meeting her eyes. He asks her to wait while he serves another customer and then pulls her aside to ask her where her family live. She is embarrassed when she mistakenly thinks he is referring to her new family, the

Vermeers, but when he corrects her she explains that her family live "Off the Rietveld Canal, not far from the Koe gate."

His eyes meet hers as he tells her about the plague, explaining that while no quarantine has been set as yet, the people in that area are expecting it soon. Griet is shocked but also realises that Pieter has been asking about her. She returns to the Vermeers in a daze, asking Catharina for permission to visit her family before they are quarantined but Catharina shows no compassion, refusing the request abruptly in concern for the risk posed to her own family. When Griet turns in desperation to Maria Thins, Catharina is aggravated and refuses Griet permission to visit her family on Sundays until the plague has completely gone.

Griet returns to her chores and is crying when Maria Thins finds her. She quietly, and with less cruelty, points out the danger but Griet is not comforted.

The next day Vermeer expresses his condolences regarding Griet's family's "misfortune". She sees kindness in his eyes so feels confident in asking for information about the quarantine. He replies in the affirmative and she changes the subject, asking why he removed the map from his painting.

His interest in her is obvious but the imagery here is quite predatory, emphasising his power over her and his ability to catch or trick her.

"His face became intent like a stork's when it sees a fish it can catch."

Griet feels brave enough to make an opinionated statement on the painting and he seems to approve of her response. His approval unsteadies her and she uses the broom to regain control. The crisis in her family provides a catalyst for a step up in the intensity of their relationship.

Q. Is Catharina being unreasonable in refusing Griet permission to visit her family?

Pages 68 – 70

Griet's housework worsens as her concern for her family increases and the Vermeer's begin to notice, Maria Thins especially telling her to steady herself. In contrast she is able to clean the studio perfectly.

On the first Sunday of the Quarantine she is at a loss as to what to do with herself, as she is unable to either go home or to her family church. She decides to visit the New Church as she was baptised there, however, she feels uncomfortable and isolated. Her inferiority is emphasised and she steps out the minute it is over.

Instinctively, she walks towards her family home knowing in her heart she will not be able to go there. She is stopped by a soldier at a barrier who shrugs off her enquiries, obviously having dealt with many already. A second soldier offers to give her information in exchange for sexual favours and she berates him for trying to take advantage of her grief. He doesn't care, showing the predominant attitude towards women at that time. Returning to the Vermeer's house, she spends the rest of the afternoon and evening alone with her prayer book carefully avoiding the Catholics.

Q. Why doesn't Griet want to stay at the Vermeer's house on a Sunday?

Pages 70 –71

At the meat Market, Pieter pulls her aside to ask if she has heard any information about her family. She starts to feel unsteady with him also just as she does in close interactions with Vermeer. This shows that she is attracted to Pieter. When he realises that she has heard nothing he assures her emphatically that he will find out what is happening. She thanks him but her gratitude is tempered by the knowledge that she will owe him.

Griet looks at Pieter's hands and is turned off by the blood in the creases. She acknowledges to herself that she will have to get used to it even though it makes her uncomfortable.

She realises during that week that she is looking forward to her trip to the butchers as much as she does to cleaning the studio, although she also dreads the news that Pieter could give her. When she finally does receive the awful news that her sister Agnes is sick, it is Pieter's eyes that tell her before he physically does.

"Then one day he looked up and looked away and I knew what he would say."

For the first time, Griet uses Pieter's name when she thanks him but is frightened by the expectation she sees in his eyes.

Q. Why does Griet assume that she will owe Pieter something for his kindness?

Pages 72 – 73

Griet visits her brother Frans on her next Sunday off. The factory is outside the city walls not far from the Rotterdam gate. He is asleep when she arrives showing the exhausting nature of his work.

She finds herself comparing her tone and attitude to that of Catharina, as she is quite rude to Frans's employer, insisting that she wake Frans up. His isolation is emphasised by his complete shock when Griet tells him about Agnes, as he has heard nothing at all about the plague. His frustration at this isolation is expressed through anger and he complains bitterly about the monotony of his position. Griet begs him to think of Agnes and then requests that he attend church with her so that they can pray for their family. He agrees and the siblings spend the rest of the afternoon together, silently supporting one another but not articulating their mutual certainty that Agnes will not recover.

Q. Why are Griet and Frans so pessimistic about Agnes's chances of recovery?

Pages 73 – 77

One morning in the following week, Maria Thins asks Griet to clean away the painting setting when she cleans the studio. She explains that the painting is finished and the scene is no longer required. Griet finds it difficult to disturb the scene she has so meticulously cleaned around for weeks, so she does everything else in the room and is still standing, staring at the scene when Vermeer enters to help her move the table. He is quite abrupt with her when he sees how little she has done but she explains her reluctance and he decides to help her.
As he moves the blue cloth in one quick movement, Griet compares him to Pieter by noticing that "his hands were very clean."
Vermeer replaces the setting with the actual painting and Griet's resistance to change is seen quite clearly. She no longer finds the studio comforting and quiet and she is especially disturbed by her master's sudden activity and haste, once again assuming that she knows him well.
She is outside with Tanneke when the Van Ruijvens arrive to inspect the painting. This is the first time Van Ruijven really notices Griet and he is immediately taken with her,

requesting that she serve him wine. Catharina dismisses her as "one of the maids" and later as "nothing", in an attempt to redirect Van Ruijven's attention to the painting. It is obvious in this scene that the Vermeers are dependent on Van Ruijven's patronage. Maria Thins and Catharina make an effort with their appearance and even Vermeer is forced to be polite.

The Van Ruijvens are admiring the painting when Griet enters with the wine but Maria Thins saves her from the embarrassment of having to deal with Van Ruijven again and she is able to escape to the kitchen. The next morning the painting is gone and Griet never sees it again.

Q. What do you learn about the patron/painter relationship from this scene?

Pages 77 – 78

At the Meat Hall the next day, Griet hears news that the Quarantine has been lifted and she pushes in at Pieter's Stall so that she can be served quickly and then visit her family. Pieter fills her order and hands her a small parcel as a gift for her family.

Griet runs all the way to her parent's house aware that "only thieves and children run" but unable to pinpoint which she is.

She discovers her parents in mourning, as her sister is dead.

Q. Which is Griet as she runs to her sister's deathbed? A thief or a child? Explain your answer.

Pages 78 – 80

After her sister's death, Griet describes her life as dull. Her chores have no meaning and even the weather is melancholy as she enters a rainy Autumn.

Tanneke and Maria Thins are quite kind to her for a few days but Catharina acts as if nothing has happened. While the children do not really comprehend the reason for Griet's grief, Aleydis manages to comfort Griet without really meaning to. Cornelia stays true to form, showing a truly mean streak by offering Griet an old doll to give to her sister with full knowledge that Agnes is dead.

Griet is unable to look to Vermeer for comfort as he is away from home a lot, not having started a new painting as yet.

Griet avoids Pieter the son despite his kindness to her and seeks out the father instead. She notes how good the meat is following her loss.

On the following Sundays she quite often visits her brother, even bringing him home to see their parents, but she notes how different their family is after the loss of Agnes. Her own absence on Sundays has also confirmed for her how she no longer sees her parent's home as familiar.

"After only a few months I could describe the house in Papists Corner better than my family's."

Catharina begins her labour and Griet is glad to be sent out looking after the girls. When she returns with them, Vermeer is wearing his quilted paternity cap and is looking both proud and embarrassed. Griet is surprised at his embarrassment and makes a judgement that it is Catharina who wants all the children and that he is not really interested. She assumes that he would much rather be left alone in the studio to paint, the assumption being that he would rather be alone with Griet. She considers the relationship between them so far and her jealousy of his wife is obvious.

"I did not like to think of him in that way, with his wife and children. I preferred to think of him alone in his studio. Or, not alone, but only with me."

Vermeer announces to the children that they have a new brother, Franciscus. Griet accompanies the children into the birthing room as they all take part in a prayer of thanksgiving. She is uncomfortable with the Catholic prayer but recognises that Protestants would also make thanks for the safe arrival of a new child. She listens to Vermeer pray and doesn't even mind the Latin phrases as his voice is soothing to her.

Griet notes that Catharina looks happy for a change, but after drinking a toast to her baby she hands him straight to the wet nurse.

Tanneke and Griet must then begin preparations for the Birth Feast. They have ten days to prepare and Griet is amazed at the magnitude of the event. Two more girls are employed to help with the preparations which include cleaning everything in the whole house, even items that will not actually be seen by any of the guests. By the end of it, Griet's hands are "cracked and bleeding."

A huge order for food is made including such delicacies as pineapple and caviar. Griet once again shows her resistance to anything new by dismissing the pineapple as not tempting and not being impressed by the caviar that Tanneke lets her sample.

Throughout all the preparations, Catharina stays in bed and Vermeer is absent from the house as much as possible. Griet describes Catharina as a swan as much for her post birth serenity as her tendency to extend her long neck and snap at the maids with her "sharp beak".

Pieter the son delivers the meat order to the house and Griet is glad that her face is not red raw as it has been in the previous few days. Cornelia watches the exchange between them closely noticing Pieter's smile when he speaks to Griet. Vermeer also sees and Griet thinks he is displeased by the young butcher's attentions to his maid. Pieter is dismayed by Griet's obvious discomfort at being "caught between the two men" and she describes the whole incident as "not a pleasant feeling."

Q. Do you believe Griet's belief that Vermeer is attracted to her is justified?

Pages 86 – 87

When Griet next visits home her parents are inquisitive about the Vermeer's. Her mother wants to know about the birth and her father wants to know about the most recent painting.
Griet finds herself sharply defending Vermeer when her mother suggests that his work output is small because he is idle.
It is obvious to her parents that discussing the painter makes Griet uncomfortable.

Q. How has Griet's relationship with her father changed?

Pages 87 – 89

The guest list for the birth feast includes wealthy merchants as well as many local tradesmen, including Pieter the father who embarrasses Griet by joking that his son will be jealous that he gets to spend all afternoon with her.

Catharina is enjoying being the centre of attention wearing the ermine mantle that features in the painting. Griet finds it odd to see it on her shoulders. (Perhaps this shows that she does not think Catharina deserves such finery.)

"I didn't like her wearing it, though it was of course hers to wear."

Catharina is a gracious and merry hostess and while her husband's eyes follow her around the room as she entertains their guests, he is much more reserved.
Van Ruijven corners Griet, grabbing her and announcing to Vermeer that he should "paint her." The implication is suggestive and Griet is embarrassed but Vermeer does not rescue her, not wanting to offend his patron. Her hero instead is Pieter the father, who asks for more wine, giving her a valid excuse to escape. She thanks him and he jokes that it was worth it to hear her call him Sir.

Q. Compare the reactions of Vermeer and Pieter the father when Van Ruijven accosts Griet.

Pages 89 – 92

It is now Winter and the house becomes cold and flat. The children are bored and the baby is a very fussy one. Catharina is surprisingly patient with the baby but snappy with everyone else, including her husband.
The preparations for the feast had given Griet something to think about besides her sister, but when there is not much to do, she finds herself dwelling on Agnes's death. She is also aware that Vermeer seems distant and she is unsure whether this is because of Van Ruijven or Pieter the son. She is worried that she has offended him even though she does not know how she has. The studio

becomes a metaphor for how Griet feels, as she is aware that it is serving no purpose at the moment and therefore it provides no comfort for her either.

One morning Griet and Maria Thins find Vermeer asleep in the studio and Griet believes he is lost for inspiration. The next day she decides to clean the windows hoping that the new light will motivate him but he walks in on her as she is cleaning. When she looks over her shoulder at him he asks her to freeze and she thinks she has done something wrong. However, he gives her permission to keep cleaning so she finishes the windows, asking for his approval when they are clean. He asks her to look over her shoulder again and she does so, realising that he is studying her intently. She is pleased that he is interested in her again.

The next day the room is set up for a new painting.

Q. What is symbolic about Griet's decision to clean the windows?

1665

Pages 95 – 99

It is March, Griet's birthday month and she describes it as symbolic of her own personality.

"March was an unpredictable month when it was never clear what might happen."

She is at home on a Sunday and her father asks her to describe the painting again. The painting is of the Baker's daughter and her father notices that the girl in the painting is wearing her cap the same way that Griet wears hers.

Top Notes

While Griet is a little impatient with her father because he wants to know every detail, she tries to be fair because she knows how much he hates Winter since his blindness have accentuated all his other senses.

She has been smuggling him little treats and describes the painting process as accurately as she can but is acutely aware that he does not have the expertise of Vermeer. She also feels he is being deliberately difficult because of the loss of Agnes and gets impatient with him when he demands to know what the story behind the painting is. She impatiently retorts,

"His paintings don't tell stories."

Her father demands to know why she has not brought him a treat and to avoid the question she lies, noting that she has become good at it in the last few months.

Her mother accompanies her back to the square at the end of the day to give her some advice about Pieter the son. Basically she is told to be pleasant, to smile and not to be rude. Griet is surprised but realises what their daughter marrying a butcher could mean to her parents. Once again she is in the position of providing for her family.

The real reason Tanneke is angry with her is because she has discovered that Griet is helping Vermeer in the studio with his paintings but Griet cannot tell her parents this.

Q. Why is Griet's father so irritable?

Pages 99 – 103

Griet explains how she began assisting Vermeer. She seems pleased that it began as a result of Catharina's wish to make her life difficult. Catharina chooses to send Griet to the apothecary on a freezing cold day as no one else wishes to go outside. As she is on her way out, Vermeer sticks his head out a window and makes his own request for some painting materials. Griet is pleased at his "secret request."

Griet is also excited at the prospect of a new experience. She has never been to an apothecary's as her mother always made her own home remedies.

The apothecary doesn't remember her from the party although Griet clearly remembers him. This underlines how invisible the serving class are in this society.

She asks for medicinal ingredients for Catharina and colours to be mixed for Vermeer. The apothecary is surprised as Vermeer has never trusted anyone to pick up his painting materials before but he is kind to her, letting her sit by the fire as he prepares her order.

On her return, Griet gives her purchases to Catharina before rushing upstairs to Vermeer but in her haste neglects to be careful in front of Cornelia who has been watching and asks her father and Griet what they are doing. Vermeer thanks Griet but then turns away, ignoring his daughter and leaving Griet to explain, which she feels very uneasy about. She feels very protective of her master and when Cornelia is not satisfied with her answers she ignores her, already very aware of the inappropriateness of his request and of how Cornelia could use this information.

Cornelia gets her revenge a few days later by interfering with Griet's meager belongings. She finds the tile that Griet's father made for her and snaps it in two, effectively separating the boy and girl figures. When Griet finds the broken tile she is deeply hurt, as it seems to confirm the growing separation between her family members and her own isolation. While she does not want Cornelia to know the effect she has had on her, she weeps privately.

Q. Why is Griet so distressed about the tile?

Vermeer asks Griet to do other things for him showing his growing trust in her. However he is much more careful about his interactions with her after the Cornelia incident. Most significantly, he asks her to help with the preparation of his colours and teaches her about the intricacies of storage and care of the precious materials. On one occasion she has to buy a pig's bladder from the butcher's because this is what the most expensive colours are stored in.

One morning he asks her to stand in for the baker's daughter, as she is sick. As Griet stands in the freezing draught from the window she understands why the girl is ill.

The room is described as bright, once again explaining Griet's frame of mind. She feels as if she is learning and that he has enlightened her.

"He had opened all the shutters. I had never seen the room so bright."

When he paints her, he looks at her intently and she is embarrassed by his scrutiny. She tries to think of something else but he sees it in her face and orders her to think of nothing. Forced into inactivity, her mind returns to Agnes and other morbid thoughts. In particular, she thinks about a hanging that she has witnessed. The punishment was inflicted on a woman who had killed her daughter in a drunken rage. This reflects the violent society she lives in, one based on punishment and retribution, but it is not clear why Griet thinks of this tragic and bloody occurrence at this moment.

She then remembers the last time she saw Agnes and feels great guilt at how she snubbed her.

Vermeer is still dissatisfied and tells her she is thinking too much, suggesting she close her eyes. When she does so, she is reminded of how her father feels,

"...with the space all around him and his body knowing where it is."

When she achieves this state she feels anchored. Vermeer is happy with the result and tells her to continue cleaning.

Q. Explain the reference to the hanging. Why does Griet connect this incident to her sister's death?

Pages 106 – 108

Vermeer begins his new painting and Griet is amazed and inspired by the construction of it. She is also consumed by the feeling of being his student, as he seems to delight in explaining to her how the layers of colour take shape. There is also the hint that he is teaching her other things about her world and while her mind is opening up so is her sexuality.

"He taught me."

She describes the painting of the baker's daughter and how surprised she is by the process. She expects Vermeer to paint certain clear objects but instead he works in "patches of colour", spending a lot of time on building up false colours to get dimensions and then blocking in the layers bit by bit till the objects begin to take shape. The baker's daughter continues to pose for the painting but Griet can see little change from day to day, just,

"..areas of colour that did not make things."

This quote could be seen as symbolic of their relationship. One morning he is annoyed with Griet when she mixes a blue that he does not ask for. She feels a physical hurt from his reproach showing the extent of his influence on her and the depth of her feelings for him. He explains that while the girl's skirt is blue, there are other colours that will make up the depth and substance of that blue and he demonstrates this lesson by showing Griet the clouds outside the window. He returns again to the vegetables and the first day they met and she comprehends the difference in the white vegetables; the turnips and onions. After a few moments staring at the clouds, she can see blue and yellow and green in them and is excited at what he has taught her.

She is not only more appreciative of what she can see in the painting now, but says that the lesson makes her see colours in everything. He has effectively changed her life as she admits,

"After that I could not stop looking at things."

Q. Describe the relationship between Vermeer and Griet to this point. Why is Griet so excited by the colours?

Pages 108 – 111

Griet and Vermeer enter the next stage of their relationship, as Griet again symbolically enters another room. Vermeer takes Griet to the attic where he grinds his paints using various tools including a grinding stone.
As he shows her how to grind the colours he places his hands over hers and she is shocked by his touch, dropping the stone. He takes his hands away and explains how she should be more effective.

"He did not try to touch me again."

Griet's naivete is evident as she explains how she feels after his touch. Her desire to please him and her description of how she grinds the precious material could be transferred to a description of lovemaking.

"I was clumsy and flustered from his touch. And I was smaller than him and unused to the movement I was meant to make."

Vermeer also shows his complete ignorance of her situation as he explains to her that the ivory she must grind is the same as the ivory comb she would wear in her hair. She does not point out that she could never afford such luxury.

Griet is more concerned at this stage that the new work will take a lot of time and she must explain to the other women in the house where she is, but when she looks to him to take care of that he only says he will consider it. She waits for him to speak to his wife but once again he does nothing.

Q. Does Vermeer show any concern for Griet when he asks her to complete extra duties?

Pages 111 – 114

The solution to this problem comes unexpectedly from Tanneke who is having trouble sleeping due to the wet nurse's snoring. She wants Griet's room so Vermeer suggests that Griet be moved to the upstairs storeroom and Catharina reluctantly agrees.

The move means that Griet becomes a captive in the studio at night, which she does not like but once again the decision is out of her hands and she must do as she is told. Ironically, it is the fact that she is able to lock Griet away at night that convinces Catharina that it is a good idea.

Griet notes that Catharina looks quite beautiful when she smiles and is a bit jealous when Vermeer invites his wife into the studio. She is wearing a wide, white collar and the next day it is included in the painting of the baker's daughter. Vermeer seems to be able to manipulate all the women in his life for the sake of his art.

Q. Why is Catharina invited into the studio?

Pages 114 – 117

Griet becomes an accomplished liar as she invents excuses to go to bed early in order to get all the work done that Vermeer has left for her. He leaves her with greater responsibility but makes no attempt to relieve her from her other duties, expecting her to somehow work it out for herself.

Despite these difficulties, Griet enjoys working with the colours and becomes more skilled at it every day. For a few moments in her hard working day she feels as if she is creating something magical.

Vermeer does not trust her completely as he does not allow her to mix the blues because of how expensive the lapis lazuli is.

Working along side of him becomes a pleasure and they both seem to be at peace during these times. Their similar natures are evident, as they are both quiet perfectionists. The intimacy of the act of mixing the paints once again seems to reflect an almost sexual act.

"When we were done we poured water from a pitcher over each other's hands and scrubbed ourselves clean."

Despite this closeness, Vermeer seems completely immune to any of Griet's physical needs. She is cold in the attic but he does not light the fire unless he is in the room. She notices that she feels warm when he is present and this is not the first time she has mentioned the heat between them.

Maria Thins is not easy to fool however. She notices that Griet is absent from the main house quite often and one day she traps Griet in the attic and demands to know what she is doing there. Griet does not know how to defend herself and Vermeer offers no assistance. However, Maria Thins proves to be practical as usual. She realises that Vermeer has been working more efficiently lately and understands that this is because of Griet's assistance. She agrees to keep the secret.

Q. How does Maria Thins catch Griet and Vermeer out?

Pages 117 – 122

Griet enjoys her new life. She feels protected by Maria Thins and Vermeer and she feels superior to the other women in the house, as she is in an upstairs room and has a view of Delft outside her window. She is isolated, which she likes and she gets to spend a lot of time with Vermeer alone.

The connection between them is growing and Griet allows herself to dream of what it would be like to be in a relationship with Vermeer as she sits alone in the studio at night, wrapped in a blanket, studying the paintings by moonlight or candlelight. Her youth and inexperience in matters of love are conveyed through her idea of what the relationship would be like. She imagines herself wearing Catharina's clothes and usurping her position as lady of the house, as she sees love as a painting and has no concept of the reality of a relationship.

For a while, Griet is able to continue her double life with the help of Maria Thins but they have both underestimated Cornelia. One day, Cornelia calls Griet and pretends to be frightened of going down the stairs. When Griet tries to help her, she spitefully throws herself at her, hurting her and then laughing.

Cornelia has asked Tanneke to get Griet to fix her collar but this is a ruse so that Tanneke can notice the red colour that Cornelia has purposely smeared on Griet's apron. Tanneke is ready to tell Catharina but Griet asserts herself and directs her to Maria Thins instead. This causes a rift between the maids as Tanneke cannot forgive Griet for speaking down to her or for having any kind of relationship with her mistress.

From then on, Tanneke never speaks kindly to Griet and goes out of her way to make life hard for her. Griet is unable to take anything nice to her parents from Tanneke's kitchen and she cannot speak about the deplorable situation she has found herself in.

All she has left to talk about is the paintings.

Q. Why does Griet speak so condescendingly to Tanneke?

Pages 122 – 125

On one occasion while she is out on the street, Griet runs into Pieter the son and he walks with her to the Apothecary's. He notices how tired she is and complains that her employers are working her too hard. This is obviously true as Tanneke is purposely making life difficult for Griet and Vermeer is taking advantage of his position and creating extra work for her to complete. Griet refuses to blame Vermeer however.

When Griet lays the blame for her exhaustion at the feet of Tanneke, Pieter explains how loyal the older maid is to the family. He recounts the story of Catharina's brother Willem, whose violence against his sister provoked an act of great loyalty on Tanneke's part. Griet also finds out that Catharina's father was a violent man and that Maria Thins was a victim of this violence.

For the first time Griet seems to attempt to have compassion for Catharina and her past suffering. She remembers how Catharina reacted when the knife dropped to the floor on their first meeting and seems to doubt her own judgement of the woman. It also occurs to her that it was left to Tanneke to defend Catharina and Griet wonders where her husband was at the time of the attack.

Pieter is sympathetic when she seems confused, gently touching her arm and moving on.

Q. Why is Griet confused?

Pages 125 – 126

On Griet's next Sunday off, she is attending church with her parents when Pieter the son slips in. This confirms for Griet that he is Protestant, something she had wondered about and obviously sees as important.

Her mother sees Pieter staring at Griet and tells her to bring him over to meet them after the service. Griet reluctantly does so; first inquiring about what he is doing there. Her repeated questions show her embarrassment. Pieter shows no embarrassment in contrast. He admits readily that he is there to see her and to meet her parents and his intentions are quite obvious.

Griet pleads with him to wait, reminding him that she is only seventeen and not ready for "such things." The real reason for her hesitation lies in her memory of Vermeer's hand over hers and she contrasts this memory with the sight of Pieter's blood stained hands.

However, she is flattered by the attention, admitting that Pieter is handsome and later, that many other young girls at the church seem to be trying to get his attention.

In response to his request to meet her parents, she leads him to them even though her father is shy of meeting strangers and not nearly as enthusiastic as her mother is about meeting Pieter.

Q. Why is Griet upset by her father's statement that he has already lost her?

Pages 126 – 131

From then on, Pieter regularly visits Griet's church and she is conscious of looking presentable. Her father even begins to 'look' for him each week. Pieter has used his charm and good manners to win Griet's parents over. He always greets them before speaking to Griet and eventually they chat easily to him, even leaving a few moments when the young couple can be alone.

Griet also begins to feel more comfortable chatting with Pieter although they consciously avoid topics such as Vermeer or his paintings. Griet especially chooses not to tell him about her extra duties.

Despite her growing affection for Pieter, Griet often finds herself feeling confused, as she wants to listen to Pieter but finds her mind wandering off onto Vermeer.

After a year of employment, Griet's mother invites Pieter to have Sunday lunch with them. Once again, Griet is taken aback by her mother's decision but realises that this is the done thing and that it would seem rude not to invite him. She is also aware of the hardship the lunch will place on her parent's meager meal allowance for the week. The tradeoff however is that if Griet marries the butcher they will always eat well.

On the first Sunday lunch, her mother wisely serves fish but after that Pieter becomes a regular visitor and he always brings gifts of meat. Griet is impressed by Pieter's good manners at the first lunch as he offers genuine compliments on her mother's cooking and asks her father about the tiles on display. Griet's father mentions the 'best tile' but Griet manages to divert attention from it, not having told her family about Cornelia's malicious vandalism.

Griet's attitude towards Pieter at this stage is ambiguous as she feels trapped in the deal being made concerning her but at the same time recognises his innate goodness. She is softening towards him but ironically feels like a piece of meat.

Her mother allows her to walk Pieter to the canal after every visit and on one occasion he guides her into a small alleyway where he kisses her eagerly. She stops him as he attempts to remove her cap and he then teases her about her hair. This conversation conveys her confusion as she lies to him about her hair because it represents her repressed emotions. Her hair is actually long and curly and "could not be tamed". She feels like a certain type of girl with her hair down and this frightens her.

Q. Explain Griet's reluctance to show her hair?

Pages 131 – 134

Vermeer finishes the painting of the Baker's Daughter. The changes he makes do not shock Griet as they used to, now that she feels as if she is more in tune with him. Once again, he allows her to look through the camera obscura;

"I came to admire the scenes the camera painted inside itself, the miniature reversed pictures of things in the room. The colours of ordinary objects became more intense."

She is concerned however, that despite her best efforts, Vermeer is still not painting faster. Her position seems to be at stake as Maria Thins may feel she is superfluous. But in fact, Maria Thins makes allowances for his other commitments and protects Griet's new position.

The baker comes to inspect the painting, bringing his whole family. Maria Thins is disappointed in the baker's simple response to the portrait but Griet sees it as an honest appraisal of the work, in contrast to Van Ruijven's over the top but fake exaltations.

Cornelia starts a game with the baker's children that is obviously designed to challenge Griet's authority. Griet is concerned about the girl's motives but when she checks her belongings later, nothing is missing.

Q. What kind of man is the baker? Use evidence from the text to back up your answer.

Pages 134 – 135

A new painting begins in July. Van Ruijven has requested a painting of his wife with her face looking at the painter. Maria Thins and Catharina discuss the fact that Vermeer does not really like to use that pose and laugh disdainfully about the last girl who was asked to pose in that way. This was a painting with Van Ruijven and a maid wearing a red dress and the inference made is that it ruined the girl's reputation.

Griet is curious so she later asks Pieter about the scandal. He also laughs, remembering how Van Ruijven asked the girl to dress in his wife's red dress, made sure there was wine in the painting that the maid was encouraged to drink and then got her pregnant by the time the painting was finished.

Griet is horrified, realising what could happen to her but she pretends nothing is wrong in front of Pieter.

Q. Why doesn't Griet tell Pieter about her fears?

Pages 135 – 138

When Van Ruijven's wife arrives, Griet is ordered to fetch Catharina's yellow mantle, pearl necklace and earrings. Catharina is out so Griet must ask Maria Thins to fetch the finery.

Vermeer's fastidious attention to detail is obvious as he gets Griet to help him set up for the painting. She helps Van Ruijven's wife into her red dress and is then sent to fetch Catharina's powder brush and then to promptly return it when he rejects the idea. Griet is obviously at Vermeer's beck and call.

Griet is fascinated by the ability of Van Ruijven's wife to sit and pose without thinking about anything, as she herself was unable to do. She also feels very connected to the painting process by this stage as she does not feel comfortable leaving until Van Ruijven's wife is released.

Q. What is Griet tempted to do while assisting Vermeer?

Pages 138 –140

Van Leeuwenhoek arrives the next day with the camera obscura. Van Ruijven's wife is unable to attend so Griet must sit in for her. Van Leeuwenhoek is surprised at her involvement in the painting process, but as usual, treats her kindly and with respect.

Griet is surprised when he bows for her and she smiles in return. He jokes with her about learning to paint but Vermeer is not in a jocular mood and orders Griet to sit as his model.

When Vermeer asks Griet to pick up a quill, she is anxious that he will ask her to write something and she is conscious of her inability to write anything but her own name.

The two men study Griet through the camera obscura, which she finds easier to stand, as they are not staring directly at her. When they are finished, they seem to forget that she is in the room and begin discussing Guild business. Van Leeuwenhoek reminds Vermeer that Griet is still sitting and suggests she be released. As Griet leaves she notices the pity on the older man's face.

Q. Why does Van Leeuwenhoek pity Griet?

Pages 140 – 144

The camera obscura is left behind for a few days and Griet takes the opportunity to look through it on a number of occasions. She does not feel comfortable with the arrangement on the table.

"It was like looking at a painting that has been hung crookedly."

While Van Ruijven's wife is there, it occurs to Griet that the scene is too neat and she decides in her mind what she would change if it were up to her. She waits several days for him to realise but Vermeer makes no changes. Griet becomes obsessed with the problem, even getting out of bed in the middle of the night to look at the scene. When Vermeer begins to block in colours, she realises she must make the change herself.

The next day when she is cleaning, she adjusts the blue cloth so that it reflects the contours of Van Ruijven's wife's arm. She acknowledges in her mind that she could be fired for her interference but is satisfied that she has done right by the painting.

For a few days she purposely avoids her work in the attic. Tanneke notices her anxiety and comments on it, even though she rarely speaks to her now.

Tanneke almost forgets that she is ignoring Griet until Griet attempts to prompt her into speaking about Catharina's brother. However, the older maid remembers her anger and reminds Griet that she is isolated and unwanted in the house.

Tanneke abuses Griet for being rude to Vermeer when he arrives, as she is unable to meet his eyes. Griet can only think of his reaction to the change she has made and the possible consequences run through her mind as she waits. He shows no reaction when he sees her later that day and in fact does not even look at her. However, when Griet goes to bed, she notices that the cloth is as she placed it and the change has been sketched into the painting. She feels validated and pleased with herself.

"I lay in bed that night smiling in the dark."

Later he watches her as she cleans the studio, studying the way she measures objects so as to exactly replace them in the correct spot. He asks her about the change she made. When she explains her reasons he admits to learning something from her, but categorises her in her place as a maid.

"I had not thought I would learn something from a maid."

Q. Why does Griet make the change to the scene?

Pages 145 – 150

On her next visit to her parent's house, Griet describes the new painting to her father as her mother and Pieter listen. Pieter is always silent when Griet talks about Vermeer. Griet leaves out the change that she made but her mother recognises how closely Griet is getting involved in the paintings and makes a comment on Vermeer's subject matter.

Frans is also present and Griet has become aware that he is becoming increasingly obsessed with material things as a consequence of his abject poverty and despair.

Griet's mother points out that Griet speaks about her master's paintings almost reverentially in a city where paintings are plentiful.

"I think his paintings are not good for the soul."

Griet reacts spitefully but immediately regrets her comment about supporting her parents. Pieter is also ashamed of her comment, spending little time with her that day.

Griet's mother points out how much Griet has changed since working for the Vermeers and while she is stung, Griet knows what her mother says is true.

Looking at the painting the following day, Griet is unable to separate the painting from its connotations and finds it painful to view. She notices that Vermeer is in a good mood so she asks him about the paintings.

"Are your paintings Catholic paintings?"

Vermeer's answers are cryptic; using questions to further confuse her but eventually he explains how a person's context affects what they see and how they understand. He points out that if her mother has not seen the painting, then it is impossible for her to tell Griet what it means. While Griet is satisfied with this answer she is also unhappy that he seems to be criticising her mother. Their discussion becomes a religious one where he explains that his paintings are not Catholic or Protestant but simply a way to see God, a way to see something holy. As Vermeer talks, Griet admits to being swayed by his argument even though her years of Protestant upbringing revolt against what he says. His words and his actions seem to have an almost hypnotic effect on her and she explains it in an interesting way considering the content of their conversation.

"I was bewitched by the movement of the silvery knife in the creamy white paint."

Vermeer admits to converting to Catholicism in order to marry Catharina and Griet is shocked. She has never heard of anyone choosing not to be Protestant and is aware of the sacrifice he has made in order to be with Catharina. She is also acutely aware of her own religious compatibility with Vermeer and this becomes another point of resentment against her mistress.

Q. Explain Vermeer's statement. "It's not the painting that is Catholic or Protestant...but the people who look at it, and what they expect to see."

Pages 150 – 153

Griet is aware that Catharina does not trust her and that she is extremely unhappy about her jewellery box being in the studio within easy reach of Griet. Catharina is also obviously jealous of Vermeer's attention to Griet and suspects her of tempting him.

Griet can see this old story from the other perspective as she remembers Van Ruijven's pursuit of the maid in the painting.

Maertge has become closer to Griet in the past months; probably filling the gap that Agnes's death has created for Griet. Maertge tells Griet about a conversation she has overheard. Catharina has demanded that her jewellery box be returned, afraid that Griet will steal it and its contents, escape out a window and make a better life for herself.

In her own childish way, Maertge is attempting to warn Griet of the impending changes in the house. The wet nurse will leave soon and Catharina wants Griet to move back downstairs, however Vermeer has not committed to anything yet.

Griet sees Catharina's request as a challenge to her husband, to choose between his wife and Griet. She knows she cannot win because he wants the jewellery box in the painting and the painting takes precedence over both his wife and her. Knowing she must return downstairs, she suddenly sees her life of servitude stretching out before her with no respite. She feels desperate, realising that life in the house will be unbearable if she cannot be near Vermeer or work with the colours.

When she arrives at the Meat Market, she is distressed to find Pieter absent, showing that she has come to depend on him. She realises that she sees Pieter as an escape and in her disappointment is rude to his father. Pieter's father continues to tease and joke with her but puts her in her place by reminding her that she will be serving meat from that stall herself soon.

Maertge is shocked at the prospect of Griet leaving the family and Griet appeals to Pieter the father never to speak to her in that way, in front of a family member again. He agrees but warns her to "get used to the flies."

Q. Why is Griet so convinced that she will be returning downstairs?

Pages 153 – 158

Vermeer comes up with a compromise that gives Griet renewed belief that he cares for her. He manages to keep Griet in the attic but returns Catharina's belongings to her each night. Each morning Catharina retrieves them from her locked cupboard and hands them reluctantly to Griet to be rearranged on the table in preparation for the day's painting.

Catharina watches Griet measure out the setting but does not dare to ask her what she is doing. It is obvious that Griet seems to have more power and authority than her mistress does while in the studio.

Cornelia has also heard about the dilemma and decides to take advantage of the situation in order to get back at Griet. She suggests to her mother that she wear her tortoise shell combs in her hair but when Catharina tries to do so she finds one is missing.

Catharina's first reaction is to blame Griet for the missing comb but Griet denies any knowledge, instantly suspecting Cornelia of implicating her. Tanneke helps spread suspicion pleased that Griet is in trouble.

In an unpleasant stand-off, Catharina must send Griet into the studio to fetch her jewellery box after Griet suggests that the comb is probably still in there.

While Catharina is downstairs searching, Griet notices Cornelia's sly presence and climbs the stair to the attic (and Vermeer) to see if Cornelia has hidden the missing comb amongst Griet's belongings.

She unwraps her grandmother's tortoise shell comb and realises that her comb has been replaced with Catharina's.

She again confirms her disdain for her mistress by comparing the quality of the combs.

"It was finer than my grandmother's, but not so much finer."

Griet is as much upset by the predicament she finds herself in, as she is about the knowledge that she may never see her treasured heirloom again. Vermeer notices her distress and she boldly asks for his help.
After Vermeer speaks to his wife and to Maria Thins, Cornelia's things are searched and the comb is found inside the shell that the baker had brought for the children, weeks earlier. This shows Cornelia's penchant for Machiavellian planning as she has waited patiently for her opportunity to get back at Griet.
Cornelia is punished severely by Maria Thins who later visits Griet in the attic. She warns Griet that while she has won a victory in this instance, she should be aware that both Catharina and Cornelia hate Griet even more because Vermeer has taken her side against them. Griet protests her innocence and asks what Vermeer has said about her. Maria Thins rebukes her, quite rightly telling her to remember her place and to "not flatter herself."
While Griet is heartened by the fact that Vermeer has criticised his wife in order to defend her and that Catharina is now aware that Griet is assisting her husband, she is also shocked to learn that Catharina is pregnant again. She covers her surprise by saying that the family is suffering financially but it is obvious she is jealous of Vermeer's intimacy with his wife.
Griet returns the comb to her mother for safekeeping but does not explain why.

Q. Why does Maria Thins say Vermeer has dealt with his wife cleverly?

Catharina's attitude towards Griet changes after the comb incident. Instead of making things difficult for her, she constantly avoids the maid, seeming to fear her. She has also taken Vermeer's words to heart concerning the children and spends much more time with them.

Maria Thins is much kinder to Griet perhaps understanding how her work is helping Vermeer to paint better and faster. Tanneke follows her mistress's lead and also softens towards Griet, making the younger girl feel as if she has won.

Cornelia does not change but she is watched more closely and Griet feels it wise to avoid contact with the girl and hide anything that could be used against her in the future. Vermeer does not seem to change in his attitude towards Griet but when she tries to thank him for her help, he bluntly dismisses it.

"When I thanked him for speaking up for me he shook his head as if shooing away a fly that buzzed about him."

Griet feels indebted to him and once again shows her hatred of owing others. She is disappointed that he did not stand up for her more vocally and that he allowed Maria Thins to explain to his wife how important Griet was to his work. She admits how much she wants Vermeer to support her.

"I had wanted him to tell Catharina himself...that he supported me...That is what I wanted."

Q. Is Griet's desire for Vermeer to support her reasonable in your opinion? Explain your answer.

Pages 161 – 164

In the following October, Maria Thins and Vermeer have a conversation within earshot of Griet about the next painting. Maria Thins is concerned about finances and tells Vermeer that he must suggest to Van Ruijven that he needs another, larger painting with more figures in it. Vermeer is worried that Van Ruijven will want Griet to be in the painting but Maria Thins dismisses the problem, more concerned about the fact that they are in debt.

Van Ruijven and his wife come to inspect the painting and Griet helps Vermeer prepare for the inspection.

Maria Thins shows her desperation by arranging for Griet to serve dinner while the Van Ruijvens are present, practically using the girl as bait to lure the patron into ordering another painting. Vermeer is not impressed but Van Ruijven greets Griet enthusiastically.

Griet is polite but tries to avoid his amorous attentions. Van Leeuwenhoek, who is also present, notices everyone's reactions and is once again very kind to Griet. Tanneke is also surprisingly helpful, making most of the trips to the dining room to save Griet's embarrassment. Van Ruijven watches her constantly however.

They discuss a possible new painting and Maria Thins suggests a concert scene. Van Ruijven says he wants to be in the next painting and Catharina happily agrees making a connection between Griet and the maid in the red dress.

Q. What does Catharina want for Griet?

Pages 164 – 171

Griet's mother has heard gossip in the market place that Griet is to be painted, so she asks her daughter about it on her next Sunday visit.

Griet pleads innocence, saying that she has not been told of this.

The next day, Pieter the father seems quite angry at her, admitting he has also heard the rumour and that his son is quite jealous. Griet demands to know what he has heard and he quietly tells her he has heard the news from Van Ruijven's cook. She once again asserts her innocence.

After giving Vermeer a few days to confirm the news, Griet finally asks Maria Thins what is to happen. Maria Thins replies with a question about how Griet would feel if she were to be painted. Griet boldly states that Van Ruijven's intentions are not honourable and Maria Thins agrees, explaining that Vermeer has defended Griet and risked his patron's anger by refusing to paint her in such a way. However, Maria Thins also reminds Griet that Vermeer may not be able to hold Van Ruijven off indefinitely as he cannot afford to risk his family's future and offend him. She suggests Griet should stop worrying and ignore the rumours.

Griet however feels that she should explain to Pieter, showing that she feels some sort of responsibility towards him. She seeks him out at the Beast Market to explain to him that the gossip is not true. Pieter is concerned because he knows that Van Ruijven is a powerful man and Griet has little power to stop him getting what he wants. Griet reluctantly tells him that Vermeer has saved her for the moment and Pieter reacts jealously. However he is gentle when he kindly reminds her of her position. He offers her a choice confirming that she would not be in servitude if she married him, but Griet continues to use the excuse of being too young to marry.

Privately, she concedes that she is concerned about how long Vermeer and Maria Thins can hold off Van Ruijven.

Q. Why does Griet seek out Pieter to explain the rumours?

Pages 171 – 173

Musical instruments begin arriving at the Vermeer's house in preparation for the concert painting. Griet stands downstairs listening to Catharina play the harpsichord for her husband. Apparently, musical instruments are one of the things that Catharina complains about not being able to afford.

In response to Griet's question, Tanneke explains that Vermeer never paints his own wife because she cannot sit still long enough.

Maria Thins sends Griet on lots of errands and allows her to visit her parents while Van Ruijven is at the house posing. Griet is astounded at the power this obnoxious man has to make all of them act differently. She uses the visit to her mother to dispel the gossip, as in front of her mother's guest she announces that a new painting has begun and everyone who is to be in it is at the house at that time.

Q. What effect does Van Ruijven have on the Vermeer household and why?

Pages 173 – 177

Griet notices that Vermeer is out of sorts and studies the painting setting to gain clues to his mood. She asks Maertge about Van Ruijven and is informed that he has brought his seventeen-year-old daughter to sit in the painting. Griet sees the girl as a substitute for herself until Van Ruijven manages to get Griet into the room.

Once again, Maria Thins sends Griet out but Griet decides to visit her brother instead of her parents, not wishing to alarm them.

When she arrives at the tile factory, everyone is reluctant to answer her enquiries and when she finds Frans, she is alarmed to find he has not been moved on to the next stage of his apprenticeship, but is still working the kiln. He tells her he is being punished for making sexual advances on the boss's wife and tells her not to judge him when she at least has the chance of a better life with Pieter.

Griet confides in her brother her problem with Van Ruijven and Vermeer, but Frans sees through her story and recognises the attention she has been shown by Vermeer. Griet is unable to deny her feelings when confronted by the reality of her desire for her employer.

"I opened my mouth but no words came out."

Q. Why is Griet not able to hide her feelings from her brother?

Pages 177 – 180

Griet returns to Papist's Corner flustered and too early, running into Vermeer and Van Ruijven on their way out. Van Ruijven demands to know if she has been purposely avoiding him and then reminds Vermeer of a promise he has made.

"My master jerked his head like a puppet."

Griet can see that Vermeer is very angry but also recognises the limited extent of his power in this situation. The next day she discovers what the conversation was about. Vermeer calls her to the studio and asks her to sit in front of the painting "The Procuress'.

Griet must sit in a different chair to the one she expected and he asks her to look over her shoulder, directly into his eyes. As she does so she is mesmerised until he calls her by her name and she realises that he is going to paint her.

Q. What is the significance of the painting, 'The Procuress' to this scene?

1666

Pages 183 – 186

On following visits to her parents, Griet's father recognises the smell of linseed oil on his daughter but lacks the confidence to guess the implications. Her mother recognises the growing distance between them but cannot understand what has happened to the old Griet. This shows the influence Vermeer has had on Griet and how much she has changed as a result of her interactions with the older man.

Griet longs to tell her parents that she is being painted but cannot, so she shifts suspicion from herself by describing the other painting. When she tells her father that Van Ruijven is being painted from the back, he is greatly amused; loving the fact that this rich man cannot actually play the instrument well and so must have his lack of talent hidden.

Griet's growing reliance on Pieter is obvious also as she admits she is growing accustomed to his Sunday visits and actually sees him as her safety net and an alternative when her life falls apart. Her intention to show him how to remove bloodstains at some time in the future shows that she has accepted her fate.

However, she is still preoccupied with the painter and some of her comments regarding Pieter are less than complimentary.

"Pieter's touch did not always repel me."

Pieter has sensed her change of heart regarding him and she finds it harder to hold off his advances in the alleyway. However, while he explores the pleasures of her body, she finds pleasure in the colours behind his head showing that Vermeer is never far from her thoughts.

Pieter feels for her hair but she stops him worried about the different Griet that her hair represents. He warns her of his intention to speak to her father but once again Griet pleads that she is too young and asks him to wait.

Frustrated, Pieter reminds her of how much she and her family owe him but is immediately sorry and gently promises to make her happy.

After he leaves her, Griet walks along the canal, studying the thin ice that symbolically represents her life and remembering when she walked along there with her brother and sister before everything changed.

Q. How does Griet really feel about Pieter?

Pages 187 – 191

Griet is now free to work openly in the attic, as her mistress is aware of her new duties. One day Griet excuses herself from the rest of the household in order to assist Vermeer upstairs. The contrast between the chaos and noise of downstairs and the peace and solitude of the studio is emphasised.

She knocks on the studio door but Vermeer tells her in future to let herself in quietly. This shows his respect for Griet as in contrast, his wife needs to be invited into his private domain.

The silence as they work suggests to Griet an unspoken connection between Vermeer and herself but it is unclear whether this is imagined on her part.

A blank canvas confronts her and she is surprised at how calm she feels, however she becomes anxious when he hands her a letter to read, aware of her own illiteracy and not wishing to look stupid. When she looks at the page, however, it is blank. Vermeer hands her a worn book instead and then manipulates her position in a number of ways. He removes the book, has her pour wine, asks her to stand, then to sit – but is unable to find the right position in which to paint her.

They both realise that the clothes she is wearing identify her as a maid and this contradicts the image he is trying to portray. She is perturbed by the thought of wearing Catharina's clothes and suggests instead that he paint her as a maid, doing something that a maid would do. Interestingly, he dismisses this idea, preferring to paint her as herself before she became a maid.

"I will paint you as I first saw you Griet. Just you."

He places a chair near the window and Griet instinctively knows that it is her place. When he asks her to turn her head towards him she describes an almost unbearable burning while trying to meet his eyes. However, she acknowledges that he sees her as a subject and is already looking at her as if she is a painting, as he looks at the lighting effects rather than at her.

She in turn begins to see him from the other side and notes the invisible barrier that exists between them.

"As he was not seeing me, I did not see him."

Griet enters an almost ethereal space where time passes and she is very still. She finally feels that he is actually looking at her and "a ripple of heat" passes through her body. He is awakening desire in her and the sensuality of the scene is evident.

"He was painting me", holds deeper implications.

Q. Why does Griet say she does not want to be painted with her mop?

Pages 191 – 194

Another day painting and Vermeer tells Griet to pull back her cap so that he can see the line of her cheek. She is reluctant as she uses her cap to hide her emotions and is at her most emotional when in his presence.
When he tells her to remove her cap completely she bluntly refuses, pulling it back on and insisting that she does not want to taint her reputation.
Vermeer seems impatient and annoyed and his solution to the problem is to bring in a load of cloth so that she can wrap her hair in the cloth and be neither a "lady or a maid."
She is left alone to experiment but he is amused when he returns and finds that she has chosen the brown cloth and wrapped it as the old lady in 'The Procuress" has done.
She reminds him that blues and yellows were for ladies and that brown is the colour that she usually wore. This shows her awareness of her place and his ignorance of how forgetting this could affect her.
However, when he asks her to try the blue and yellow, she does and he is pleased with the effect.

Q. Why is Griet so insistent that she not be painted with her head bare?

Pages 195 – 197

Griet has promised not to look at the painting but she is dying to. She admits not wishing to hide anything from her master however, and understands that Vermeer and Maria Thins have made a deal with Van Ruijven to save Griet from having to pose with the man. The payoff for this will be that Van Ruijven will own her likeness. She doesn't like this thought and doesn't think that Vermeer is happy about it either, but they have little choice.

Van Leeuwenhoek knows about the second painting also, as he brings the camera obscura to look at her. Griet is excited to be under the scrutiny of two gentlemen.

When Vermeer leaves the room, Van Leeuwenhoek warns Griet to be careful of being caught between Van Ruijven and Vermeer and makes the accurate observation that she is a little naive about men and their intentions. He advises her that Vermeer's main interest in her stems from rivalry with his patron rather than any real emotional interest in her.

"Competition makes men possessive."

The older man almost has her convinced that while Vermeer would not intentionally hurt her, she could easily get lost in his paintings and he would not consider the consequences on others, including her. When Vermeer returns however, he comments on her movement from her place and she immediately returns, both physically and symbolically, to where he wants her to be.

"I am sorry, Sir." I took up my position once more."

Q. How valid is Van Leeuwenhoek's appraisal of the situation?

Pages 197 – 201

Catharina is six months pregnant when Vermeer starts to paint Griet and she is not very complimentary about her mistress. Griet is concerned however that Catharina will discover the painting but reassures herself with the knowledge that Catharina is so big and clumsy that she would not climb the stairs.

Van Ruijven is more of a worry as he is not able to keep a secret and often hints to Catharina about what is going on upstairs. He is often at the house and grabs Griet on a number of occasions making suggestive comments.

Griet is worried about his deliberate indiscretions to Catharina and tells Maria Thins but even she cannot stop him. He in fact sees it as a game and his behaviour worsens.

Griet thinks about the day that Catharina finally sees the painting of her maid and realises how much time her husband has spent shut up alone with the young girl, both of them staring into each other's eyes.

Q. Explain Van Ruijven's behaviour.

Pages 201 – 203

Vermeer is also working on the concert painting simultaneously and often requires Griet to stand in for the models. She feels used sometimes,

"He simply wanted a body there."

Van Ruijven frustrates Vermeer often driving him to the tavern to unwind after having to deal with him all day. Griet describes how uncomfortable holding the pose is but also how it is her favourite time of the week because his eyes are only on her. She is starting to show a possessive streak.

Her feelings for Vermeer grow as the painting does. As he takes control, she becomes more and more unsure of what he expects of her and the painting process seems to reflect their relationship.

"Then he was not like a painter, but like a man, and it was hard to look at him."

He lets her look at the painting one day because he is not entirely satisfied with it. He realises that it depicts Griet as Van Ruijven would like to see her but not the way that Vermeer sees her. When Griet looks at the painting she immediately sees what is missing but does not articulate her discovery. She recognises that the inclusion of the item will be the end of her position at the Vermeers, her relationship with the painter and her own innocence.

Q. What does Griet think is missing from the painting?

Pages 203 – 208

Even though Griet knows what the painting needs, she is not willing to give Vermeer the answer and it is Catharina who inadvertently helps her husband discover the missing element.
He is watching one day as Catharina plays with the girls. She has brought out her pearls and to encourage her good mood he asks Griet to bring his wife a glass of wine. He looks between Griet and his wife, watching the pearl earring swinging from his wife's ear and catching the light.

"It made us all look at her face and reflected light as her eyes did."

When Vermeer excuses himself to go back to work, Griet is aware that she will soon be wearing the pearl earring. The next day she feels drained while doing her chores, knowing what he will ask her and knowing that she cannot refuse his request as she was "beholden to him."

Maria Thins recognises her mood and attempts to find out what is wrong but Griet manages to evade her questions. As she enters the studio, Griet is immediately struck by his nervousness and before he has a chance to ask her, she says that she cannot do it and he responds by admitting how much she always surprises him.

The conversation becomes more sensual and Griet finds herself running her fingers over the lions head chair as he watches.

"I ran my fingers around the lion's nose and mouth and up to its muzzle to its mane, smooth and knobbled. His eyes followed my fingers."

He convinces her by telling her what she already knows, that the painting will not be complete without the earring. Griet now understands Van Leeuwenhoek's warning and is perhaps more dismayed by the fact that borrowing Catharina's earring will put her on the street. Despite her pleas he hardens himself, leaving her in no doubt that she cannot refuse him.

"I would never stop working on a painting if I knew it was not complete, no matter who was to get it."

He commands her to go and prepare herself but while she is changing she becomes aware that he is in the room. Her hair is out and he can't help but comment on it as his anger dissipates.

"'Your hair.' He said. He was no longer angry. At last he let me go with his eyes."

Q. What do you learn about the character of Vermeer from this extract?

Page 208

Once Vermeer has seen her hair, Griet feels sexually released, that she no longer has something to hide. She initiates sex with Pieter, however she thinks of Vermeer the whole time.

On her return to the studio she notices that Vermeer has added a wisp of hair to the painting.

Pages 208 – 210

Griet again tries to convince Vermeer that she does not need to wear the earring but he is determined. Griet begins to realise that he cares more about the painting than he does about what will happen to her when his wife finds out. Knowing that he is prepared to ruin her for the sake of his art she tries one last desperate measure, explaining that her ear is not pierced.

Vermeer dismisses the excuse, effectively ordering her to have her ears pierced for the painting and callously telling her to "leave her mouth open" in the painting, leaving her feeling cheapened.

Again she realises he has ruined her and is aware of her own loss of innocence.

Q. To what extent has Griet contributed to her own feelings of being cheapened?

Pages 210 – 212

Griet tries to think of someone who can help her with the daunting task of piercing her ears but can only come up with Frans. She visits the tile factory to ask for his help but finds when she arrives that he is gone.

The pregnant woman at the factory tells her in no uncertain terms that her brother has gone towards

Rotterdam. Griet is reminded of the tile that Cornelia prophetically broke and feels completely isolated.

The next day she visits the apothecary who by now knows her by name. She requests something to numb the skin, knowing that she will have to perform the task herself. He sells her clove oil in exchange for two days wages. On the following Sunday she must lie to her mother, explaining that her reduced wages is a consequence of breaking a mirror. She must take her mother's criticism and agree painfully that she has, "been very careless."

Q. Why does Griet agree with her mother that she has been very careless?

Pages 212 – 214

Later that night, Griet collects a needle, mirror and her clove oil. She can hear people moving downstairs and this makes her restless so she forces herself to sit patiently until everyone is asleep. She then makes preparations to pierce her own ear, realising her fear when she sees her eyes in the mirror. She performs the operation quickly, understanding the folly of delay.

As she faints, she remembers ironically how much she has always longed to wear pearls.

Pages 214 – 215

The pain is ongoing, as Griet is unable to wear the earring during the day and so must re-pierce her ear every evening. Her ear becomes infected and she must hide the swollen ear and her own discomfort under her cap during the day while she performs her usual chores.

Van Ruijven once again accosts her, trying to fondle her breasts and pressuring her to give in to him. Griet calls desperately for Tanneke but is unexpectedly saved by Cornelia.

Q. How does Cornelia save Griet?

Pages 215 – 223

On Griet's 18th birthday she cleans the studio, wondering about the paintings and what Vermeer will paint next. Ironically she considers the paintings of single figures uncomplicated, despite the chaos that has been created in her own life as a result of her own painting.

Maertge accompanies Griet to the meat hall and Griet hopes to use the girl as a shield between herself and the young butcher, embarrassed about what has passed between them. However, when she arrives, only Pieter the father is there. He wishes her a happy birthday, which surprises Maertge who knows nothing about it.

Griet is rude to the butcher, as usual, especially when he hints that his son has gone to Griet's father to ask for permission to marry her.

Many thoughts run through Griet's mind as she does her chores later until Maria Thins fetches her to see Vermeer. The older woman gives Griet the pearl earrings and informs her that Catharina is out for the morning, so Griet knows that she is about to be painted wearing the earrings.

When she arrives in the attic, Vermeer tells her to prepare to sit, but while she is getting ready Pieter arrives and calls her to come downstairs.

When she does so, he asks her what she was wearing on her head, obviously concerned about her closeness to the painter. She begs him to walk with her away from the prying eyes of the family, but he is stubborn and announces that he has permission to marry her and that she can leave her position at the Vermeers and come with him immediately.

Griet reacts with shame and anger, refusing to acknowledge his proposal and leaving him standing in the street as she returns upstairs. As she passes Tanneke she hears her insult, "Whore".

When she returns to Vermeer, she apologises for the interruption and prepares herself to be painted.

Vermeer shows his displeasure and questions her about whether she will leave and marry the butcher, but Griet requests that they not speak about him.

When Vermeer holds out the earring, Griet is bold enough to ask him to put it in for her. As he touches her she can barely express her emotions, describing the feeling as if she had been, "holding my breath under water."

Once again she describes the feeling as being similar to fire invoking the passion she feels for her master. Vermeer takes the opportunity to run his fingers down her cheek in one of the most sensual moments of the novel. Up to this point it may have been fair to say that Griet imagined much of the sexual tension between the two however in this scene she is validated, as the older man gives in to the temptation to touch the young girl in his charge.

The moment is instantly destroyed as Vermeer insists from his easel that Griet wear the other earring, despite the fact that it will not be visible in the painting and his full knowledge that her other ear is not pierced. Griet is distressed,

" 'Why?' I finally answered. 'It can't be seen in the painting.'"

She acquiesces and immediately pierces her other ear, wearing it with pain as he paints her. He does not allow her to tend to her other chores and when he finishes the painting, orders her to return the earrings to Maria Thins and go downstairs. Griet cries in silence as she follows his orders but she waits for a few moments in the storeroom, hoping he will come in and look at her with her hair out as he did before. When he doesn't she is forced to acknowledge,

"Now that the painting was finished he no longer wanted me."

Griet finishes undressing and enters the studio, pondering whether she should look at the finished painting. She does not, thinking she can do so later that night in her own time; however this is not to be the case.

Q. Why does Vermeer require both ears to be pierced?

Pages 223 – 229

Catharina is unaware of everything that has happened in the house when she returns and Griet has only just returned her earrings to Maria Thins.
Griet is doing laundry when she hears Maria Thins speak to her daughter in a worried tone. When Griet goes to investigate she sees the very pregnant Catharina dragging herself up the stairs towards the studio. She realises that Cornelia is leading her mother to the studio and that chaos is about to ensue. There is nothing that either Griet or Maria Thins can do to stop what is to happen and Vermeer himself is out of the house.
Griet hears raised voices as Maria Thins follows her daughter and Cornelia appears, telling Tanneke to fetch Vermeer. As Maertge is sent to get her father, Cornelia looks triumphantly at Griet who returns to her chores resignedly.

It is Cornelia who is finally sent to get Griet and she feels as if she could slap her but restrains herself. When she sees Catharina she can tell she has been crying by her tear stained red face. She is sitting in Vermeer's chair in the studio but raises herself to her full height when Griet enters the room. Maria Thins and Vermeer are also in the room but are silent.

Griet is accused of stealing Catharina's earrings even though both Maria Thins and Vermeer have full knowledge of how she came to be wearing them. While they both allow Catharina to vent her rage at Griet, neither of them wants the maid to speak, afraid of what she might say. While Catharina pretends that the main problem is Griet wearing her earrings, it is obvious she is much more upset about the idea of her husband spending all that time alone with her maid. Griet goes through the things she could say that would shift blame from her but sees no point and stays silent.

As Catharina becomes more hysterical it seems she is about to destroy the painting but Vermeer stops her before she can run the palette knife through the canvas. As the knife falls near Griet she resists the urge to pick it up as a maid should, looking intently into Vermeer's eyes before turning and walking away from the scene. She does not stop until she gets outside where she runs, acknowledging once again that, "..only thieves and children run."

When she reaches the centre of the square she faces her limited options; her parents, Pieter, even Van Ruijven amongst others. She makes her final choice, the only valid one she feels she has and walks steadily towards her new home and away from Vermeer.

Q. Assess Maria Thins and Vermeer's behaviour. Why do they not defend Griet and why do they

allow pregnant Catharina to get herself into such a state?

1676

Pages 233 – 236

It is ten years later when the story resumes and a twenty eight-year-old Griet describes the visit of a much-changed Tanneke to the meat stall where Griet works alongside her husband Pieter. Her own hands are blood- stained showing that she has accepted her place.

Tanneke bluntly tells Griet that Maria Thins wishes to see her and orders her to go to the house that afternoon. Griet is obviously annoyed at the command, acknowledging that she has not been in servitude since she left the Vermeer's.

Griet does her best to be polite to Tanneke even though the older maid still treats her as inferior. Griet inquires about her former employers but it becomes obvious during the conversation that she is aware of the death of Vermeer himself.

Griet mentions the irony of the Vermeers actually owing her something. They had switched butchers when she started working with Pieter at the meat stall and had not bothered to settle their account. Once again Pieter shows his honorable nature by not pursuing the money, seeing it as a fair price in exchange for his wife.

Griet is now a mother of two boys, Frans and Jan, and her mother is also present. (She later explains that her father has died.) People who love and care for her surround her and it seems her final choice was the right one to make. She thinks about the Vermeers. Catharina has continued to bear children after Griet's departure, a total of eleven offspring despite having lost one on the studio floor the day of the incident.

When Tanneke leaves, Griet decides to follow her request and go to the Vermeers that afternoon. She avoids her mother's questions while acknowledging that Pieter will not ask any. He has proven himself to be a good husband and has let her reserve some thoughts for herself.

Q. Does Griet have any regrets about the decision she made to marry Pieter?

Pages 236 – 239

In this section, Griet considers how her life has changed since leaving her position at the Vermeer's. She remembers how difficult it was at first to see her old master in the street and how she wondered if he still cared for her. However, the birth of her son gave her a new focus and she was finally able to determine that,

"...he had always cared more for the painting of me than for me."

She has also occasionally run into the other members of the family but they have mutually ignored each other except for Maria Thins polite nods and Maertge who openly spoke to her and brought Griet's belongings to her after her hurried departure. Maertge has also kept Griet up to date with the details of the Vermeer's lives until she herself grew up and married a silk merchant.
It was from village gossip that Griet had heard of Vermeer's death and how he left Catharina and her brood in huge debt.

Q. What information has Maertge given Griet about her family?

Top Notes

Griet scrubs her fingernails clean before visiting the Vermeer's. She thinks about how Pieter the father has teased her about the flies and the blood stains and she acknowledges how many things she has had to get used to. She also notes that her eyes are not as wide and innocent as they were.

When she arrives, she is once again greeted by children, although it is different ones to the originals. Franciscus recognises her as the girl in the painting and Griet asks where it is. He tells her that Van Ruijven died in the previous year and his daughter has the painting now. Franciscus goes on to explain that his father had asked to borrow the painting just before he died and Griet cannot help exclaim at the thought. Maria Thins enters the scene then and confirms this information. She explains that it is Catharina and Van Leeuwenhoek who wish to see Griet and tells her to go into the Great Hall.

On her agonising walk to the hall she sees Cornelia who is now about sixteen, still with the look of cunning that ruins her looks.

When she enters the room, Van Leeuwenhoek is gracious to her as always but Catharina still tries to act in a superior fashion, despite the fact she is obviously impoverished. She is angry that she must see Griet again but seems to have no choice in the matter, as Van Leeuwenhoek is the executor of Vermeer's will.

Catharina unexpectedly explains to Griet how in debt the family actually is before Van Leeuwenhoek explains to Griet why she has been summoned. Vermeer has requested that the pearl earrings are to be given to Griet and despite Catharina's reluctance, Van Leeuwenhoek is determined that his friend's wishes be carried out.

Catharina bitterly hands over the earrings, stating that she has not worn them since Griet. Griet refuses to take them but as Catharina says it is not their decision to make.

"..It's not for you to decide. He has decided for you, and for me. They are yours now, so take them."

As much as they hate each other, the women are aligned in their inability to refuse his wishes.

On the way out, Cornelia, who has been listening, suggests that Griet could give her the earrings and Griet does what she has always longed to do. She slaps her hard across the face.

Q. Is Griet right to slap Cornelia?

Pages 247 – 248

Griet cannot tell her husband about the earrings without explaining everything that went between Vermeer and herself so she trades them in at a pawnshop for twenty guilders. Five she intends to keep for herself, not to spend but as a reminder of her time with the painter; but fifteen she intends to give to Pieter as an explanation for her visit, the payment of a debt to the butcher and a chance to free herself from owing anybody anything.

"A maid came free."

Q. Explain Griet's final statement, "A maid came free."

SETTING

The city of Delft in 17th Century Holland provides the backdrop for this novel. The setting is significant because the genre of the novel is historical fiction meaning it uses real people, places and events as a starting point for a fictional story about a young girl's sexual awakening.

The Delft of the novel is accurately described as a place of significant artistic and cultural activity during the time period described. Ie, 1664 – 1676. Many talented and well respected artists worked from Delft, including Carel Fabritius who had previously studied under Rembrandt, and Pieter De Hooch, both of whom influenced Vermeer's style greatly.

However, this information relates more to context than setting. The setting of the novel is the time and place when events occur. The main settings in *Girl with a Pearl Earring* are Griet's parents' house, The Vermeer's home and The Marketplace in Delft itself.

Griet's family home is simple, clean and bare. The few furnishings are essentials and they must stay in the same spot to accommodate Griet's father's blindness. Griet must share a room with her sister and her father feels the cold in the poorly heated rooms in the Winter.

As much as she misses her family when she leaves home, it is a small step for Griet to begin preferring the home of the Vermeers with its spacious rooms, luxuries and substantially better meals. Despite it being a house where secrets could not be kept easily she notices how much she prefers the comforts it provides.

"The room too was different – no marble tiles, no thick silk curtains, no tooled leather chairs. Everything was simple and clean without ornamentation. I loved it because I knew it, but I was aware now of its dullness."

The most important room at the Vermeers according to Griet is the painter's studio. This is the only place that both Vermeer and Griet can escape to, away from the clutter and noise of the rest of the household.

"It was an orderly room, empty of the clutter of everyday life. It felt different form the rest of the house, almost as if it were in another house altogether."

The studio has whitewashed grey walls and contains only what Vermeer needs to set up and complete a painting. The room itself is almost a blank canvas that he can arrange and rearrange for inspiration. The windows are significant because they let in or shut out light and Griet often connects Vermeer with the window.

The attic above the studio is a small room with a slanted roof and a window that allows a view of the New Church. The room only contains the essentials for colour grinding, a cupboard, a small stone table and eventually Griet's belongings.

Griet often refers to action taking place outside of the main house in the courtyard. Griet hangs laundry out there and sometimes sits with the children as they play. The setting that Chevalier describes is similar to Vermeer's painting, "Street in Delft" and to other paintings of Delft painted by his contemporaries.

The centre of Delft is the Market Square and the city is connected by the canal. Few roads exist, only alleys and waterways. The canal becomes an important symbol for Griet and is synonymous with life in Holland.

The Meat Hall is south of the Market Square and "..in side were thirty- two stalls." The atmosphere is busy, loud and competitive as the butchers do their best to win business and the mainly female shoppers bargain for the best deal.

It is also a noisy place because of the gossip that passes through there. This is where Griet finds out most of the information about her own life that she was not aware of. There is a realness about the meat market that distinguishes it from the sterile environment of Griet's family home and the studio.

"Sawdust on the floor soaked up blood and clung to shoes and hems of dresses. There was a tang of blood in the air that always made me shiver."

Although it is a place of death there also exists the passion of life as the butchers ply their trade of sustaining the people of Delft with flesh and blood. Griet is disturbed by the blood- stains and the activity but recognises the life that will eventually sustain her.

Locate a map of Delft and plot all the landmarks that Griet refers to in the novel.

CHARACTER ANALYSIS

The main characters in *Girl with a Pearl Earring* are:

Griet
Vermeer
Catharina
Maria Thins
Cornelia
Pieter the son
Van Ruijven
Tanneke

You should also consider the influence of the following lesser characters:

Van Leeuwenhoek
Griet's parents
Frans
Agnes
Maertge

Chevalier cleverly paints her characters not unlike Vermeer painted his. She carefully arranges their background settings and blocks in their descriptions before painting the intricacies of their characters with meticulous brush strokes until a perfect image is formed. In your study of character, you should consider the desires and motivations of each individual character and then look closely at their interactions and conflicts with other characters. Keep in mind that you have been positioned as a reader to hear only Griet's perspective of each character. Try and consider each character's context before making judgement based only on the first person narrative. Consider the restraints that this society has placed on the character as a result of their gender, class or financial status.

Griet

"I measured each thing in relation to the objects around it and the space between them."

At the beginning of the novel, Griet describes herself as a calm girl who is not surprised easily. However, Chevalier has cleverly presented the reader with a narrator who does not know herself as well as she thinks she does and actually goes through a crisis in identity throughout the narration.

She is sixteen when she is first placed at the Vermeer's. A wide-eyed innocent who likes to wear her cap in such a way as to be able to hide her emotions. She is careful in preparation of her own appearance and is obviously attractive as she secures the attentions of a number of men in the novel.

Griet says she likes to see things the way that they really are and she is very proud, as can be seen by her relief that she has scrubbed the front step so hard, when the Vermeer's come to inspect her. She does not want anyone to think badly of either her or her family.

While she is very guarded and does not always say what she feels, she is privately quite judgmental of others. She is inclined to be critical of those she feels threatened by or whom she feels do not meet her own high standards.

She says she is truthful, "I did not often lie." However, the 'often' betrays her admission that she does misrepresent the truth on occasion, and this becomes more often as the story progresses. She admits later to becoming quite accomplished at lying but she is not able to fool either Maria Thins or her own mother. Griet is good at saying what she thinks other people want to hear. She flatters

Tanneke into a false sense of her own worth in order to get on her good side and omits certain details about her new life when she talks to her family, not wanting to upset them.

Maria Thins recognises Griet as both clever and cunning but she also has many positive attributes. She is kind and usually patient with her father, bringing him treats when she can and trying to explain the paintings in a way that he will understand. She also tries to relieve her father's guilt when he is concerned about her hands and is proud to hand over her wages to help support her family.

Griet has strong reactions to a number of characters. She detests Van Ruijven on sight and is particularly disdainful in her descriptions of Catharina. She rarely says anything positive about her mistress and her comments can be interpreted as quite catty and jealous.

One of the most interesting things about Griet is her obsessive behaviour. She is busy arranging vegetable slices in colour order when we first meet her and Vermeer recognises the same perfectionist nature in her that he has himself. She later becomes obsessed with the change she feels Vermeer must make to the painting scene and cannot sleep until the change is made. More importantly she becomes obsessed with the idea of being in a relationship with Vermeer and can think of little else, even when she is alone in the alley with Pieter.

Griet's identity crisis becomes evident in the latter stages of the novel. Her inner conflicts and her burgeoning sexuality create a fascinating character with contradictory traits. A girl who seems demure but is excited by two gentlemen staring at her. A girl who likes things to be realistic, but dreams of usurping her mistress's position. Her hair represents her repressed emotions and when Vermeer finally sees her with her hair down, she feels free to explore the hidden part of herself.

"When it was uncovered it seemed to belong to another Griet – a Griet who would stand in an alley alone with a man, who was not so calm and quiet and clean."

Question

How is Griet's ability to measure objects similar to the way she measures and judges people?

Vermeer

"When he was happy, when he was working well, he strode purposefully back and forth, no hesitation in his stride, no movement wasted...when things did not go well, he stopped, stared out the window, shifted abruptly, started up the attic ladder only to climb back down before he was halfway up."

There are many similarities between the personalities of Vermeer and Griet. Like her, he shows a meticulous attention to detail and he is obsessive about getting his paintings right. He likes the solitude and silence of the studio, finding it to be an escape from the noise and chaos of his large family. Also like Griet, he likes to hide his emotions under his large hat and shows little reaction to others, usually because he is not actually seeing them as people but as subjects.

Unlike Griet, however, Vermeer shows little concern for those close to him. He is good at manipulating the women in his household, using his charm to get what he wants but ignorant of either his wife's or Griet's positions after he has used them.

The first contact Griet has with him is through his voice and she often refers to the way he sounds throughout the novel, his low soothing voice that sounded like dark wood or cinnamon.

Vermeer is an intense and insular man. He rarely speaks, preferring to watch others. He refuses to buy into the competitive world of painting in Delft and paints at his own pace, sacrificing nothing for speed and seemingly unconcerned about his family's financial position.

Griet's father calls him a fair man and he does make a position available for Griet as a result of her father's accident. However, while he does appreciate Griet and her sensitivity to his art, he thinks nothing of her physical or emotional needs, refusing to light the fire in the attic for her and expecting her to complete an ever increasing work load. At times the imagery describing him is quite sinister and predatory.

"His face became intent like a stork's when it sees a fish it can catch."

Griet connects Vermeer with windows partly because he illuminates and enlightens her,

"When he smiled his face was like an open window."

But also because he puts up a barrier between himself and the rest of the world that he rarely crosses.

"I viewed his movements as if I were standing in the street, looking in through the window."

Van Leeuwenhoek warns Griet to be careful of Vermeer's competitive nature and she has to admit finally that he is only interested in her as a subject to be painted. His callous treatment of her as he paints her, insisting that she pierce both ears and leave her mouth open, making her feel cheapened, seems to contradict Griet's father's belief that Vermeer is "a fair man."

Question

Assess Vermeer's true feelings for Griet. Does she imagine more than he actually feels?

Catharina

"Sometimes I think she's filling the house with children because she can't fill it with servants as she'd like."

Griet is never very complimentary about Catharina but while we judge from the narrator's perspective it is not difficult to see why Catharina is suspicious of Griet. After all, her intuition is correct. The maid *is* after her husband and her husband seems to be encouraging her.

As with Vermeer, Griet's first recollection of Catharina is her voice. It is as bright as polished brass, evoking images of wealth, nervousness and cold. We later read that Catharina has had quite a violent upbringing so it is not surprising that she is highly- strung and anxious. Throughout the story, she is also often pregnant which would account for her highly emotional state.

However, Griet is not the only character who does not think much of Catharina. Tanneke treats her with little respect, calling her lazy, "Queen of the bedcovers" and advising Griet on how to get around her. Van Leeuwenhoek has little time for Catharina either and as he is a sound judge of character, this confirms Griet's opinion for the reader.

While Griet admits that Catharina is quite beautiful when she is smiling, she rarely is in a happy mood and this makes her seem sour and sulky. She uses a harsh tone with her servants and shows no compassion for Griet when her family is affected by the plague, either before or after Agnes's death. She dismisses Griet as a silly girl and in front of Van Ruijven, as "nothing."

Catharina likes being the centre of attention. She is a gracious and merry hostess at the birth feast because entertaining displays her status.
She is superficial and enjoys the trappings of wealth,

"...wearing her pearls and yellow mantle always made her happy."

She ignorantly wants her husband to paint faster so that she can have luxuries like musical instruments and jewels but is not allowed into his studio because of her clumsiness.
Despite Griet's harsh appraisal of her, some images portray a quieter Catharina, content just to be with her children, doing their hair or teaching them to sew.
By the end of the novel, it is clear that Catharina and Griet had more in common than they realised as both are still at the mercy of the man who controlled and manipulated them.

Question

Why does Catharina keep having children?

Maria Thins

"She was the kind of old woman who looked as if she would outlive everyone."

Maria Thins is the matriarch of the Vermeer household. It is her home and she holds the financial purse-strings even though it is Vermeer who provides the cash flow.
Maria Thins has intense blue eyes and grey curly hair. Griet notes that her teeth are stained from her pipe smoking and her hands from ink but apart from this she is immaculately dressed. She seems stern and indeed she

takes no nonsense, seeing through Griet's attempts at flattery but she also appreciates having someone intelligent in the house and, for the most part, is amused at the trouble Griet causes.

Maria Thins is quite fair to Griet. She shows compassion when Agnes dies and tries to shield Griet from Van Ruijven's presence. She appreciates Griet's work ethic and covers for her when she is assisting Vermeer with the colours. However she often rebukes her when Griet lets her guard down and says something inappropriate about Vermeer. Maria Thins is aware of Griet's feelings for Vermeer but allows the close contact to continue as she feels it will make her son-in-law paint faster.

Like all of Chevalier's characters, Maria Thins has a more negative side. She does not defend the servants against her daughter's harsh treatment and in a particularly disturbing moment, seems willing to use Griet as bait for Van Ruijven's continued patronage. Griet becomes increasingly aware that she cannot look to Maria Thins to protect her.

"It became clear to me that in spite of her shrewd ways, Maria Thins was soft on the people closest to her. Her judgement was not as sound as it appeared."

Question

Explain why Maria Thins doesn't speak up for Griet when Catharina discovers the painting.

Cornelia

"She could be funny and playful one moment, then turn the next, like a purring cat who bites the hand stroking it."

Cornelia is a thoroughly nasty little girl. It is difficult to believe that a seven-year-old could be so Machiavellian. Griet often connects Cornelia with the cat because of her changeable nature. She is able to turn on the charm when she wants to manipulate others, (as her father can), but has the capacity for great cruelty (not unlike her mother.) In fact Cornelia seems to have inherited the worst traits of each of her parents.

She immediately challenges Griet and when she is slapped as a consequence, begins a vendetta so intense that Griet cannot let her guard down for a moment. Her plans are so well thought out and meticulously carried though that Griet has little chance to avoid them. Cornelia can be cruel when bored as can be seen when she laughs at her brother's distress when his toy rolls into the fire. However it is more than boredom that prompts her pursuit of Griet. She is unbelievably cruel in the face of Griet's grief after Agnes's death and takes pleasure in physically hurting her when she jumps from the attic stairs.

Griet makes the point that Maertge was also capable of yelling at Griet when angry. In contrast, Cornelia was impassive, insidiously waiting for her opportunity and hoarding information that she can use against Griet at a later time.

"It was in her nature to be sly, to slip away when no one was looking."

Griet believes that Cornelia has no valid reason for disliking Griet, besides a "vague mistrust." But she is obviously jealous of the attention Griet gets from Vermeer as she craves her father's notice and rarely gets it. Her hatred worsens when her father takes Griet's side over hers in the comb incident and as she is punished by Maria Thins she refuses to cry.

Question

Why does Cornelia hate Griet so much? How do you feel about her when Griet sees her again at age sixteen?

Pieter the son

"He was a handsome man, even I could see that with his long blond curls, bright eyes and ready smile."

Pieter is not only handsome; he is good, kind and generous. His good looks make him a little arrogant and he tends to try and charm Griet at first before he realises her true nature and wears her down by being what she needs. A dependable, stable alternative to the turmoil she is experiencing at the Vermeer's.

Griet is worried that a deal is being made above her head when the two butchers first see her, but she gets used to the idea of Pieter being around as he continues to visit her church and ingratiate himself with her family. This is mainly because of his good manners and the respect he shows her family, despite their impoverished state. However, Griet finds it hard to respond to Pieter's affections. Her first recollection of him is interesting.

"His eyes came to rest on me like a butterfly on a flower and I could not keep from blushing."

This image suggests gentleness and genuine appreciation but also the idea of a bee feeding off an innocent flower that has no choice in the process at all. This sums up Griet's attitude to Pieter throughout the novel. She is attracted to him and often refers to his goodness and generosity, his compassion when her family were affected by the plague. However she is not always complimentary, repelled by his blood stained hands and resenting the debt she owes him.

Pieter is genuinely concerned about Griet's welfare and is worried that the Vermeers are working her too hard. He is determined to have her and patiently goes about his plan to make Griet his wife. He is playful and charming and genuinely wants to make her happy.

On the whole, Griet's description of Pieter is usually positive despite her reservations about him. He is after all, the man she chooses to marry.

Question

What does Griet have to offer Pieter? Why does he want to marry her so badly?

Van Ruijven

"He smiled as if he were about to pay a flattering but false compliment."

There is nothing pleasant about this man. He is ostentatious in his appearance and flaunts his power and wealth with full knowledge of the effect he has on others. He speaks in a derogatory manner to his wife and uses his seventeen-year-old daughter as a stand in, in the painting, for the girl he would like to sleep with, Griet.

He is ungracious in his knowledge of how dependant the Vermeers are on his patronage and Griet quite rightly states that he has no real appreciation for art, his comments are over the top and superfluous.

"Van Ruijven tried too hard when he looked at paintings, with his honeyed words and studied expressions. He was too aware of having an audience to perform for."

Van Ruijven is able to manipulate Vermeer like a puppet and is pleased when he sees the effect his desire for Griet is having on the painter. He enters into the competition eagerly, taunting the nervous and heavily pregnant Catharina with hints that her husband is cheating on her. Griet's first impression of Van Ruijven is an accurate and lasting one. He is plump, with a moustache and an 'oily smile'. He wears a long white feather in his hat that shows his love for the trappings of wealth.

Van Ruijven has already been guilty of destroying one maid's reputation and life. He feels no guilt however and is willing to repeat the process with Griet. In fact one of the things he loves about her as he tries again and again to accost her is her wide-eyed innocence and naivete about the reality of sex. Van Ruijven is a thoroughly detestable character.

Question

Does Van Ruijven have any good qualities? Find two quotes to support your answer.

Tanneke

"Tanneke was a simple creature underneath and wanted an easy time of it."

Tanneke is twenty- eight years old when Griet arrives at the Vermeer's and has been working for Maria Thins for fourteen years. Griet describes her as having a broad face with a bulbous nose, thick lips and scars from a previous illness. Griet concedes however that she has nice eyes.

"Her eyes were light blue, as if she had caught the sky in them."

Griet immediately enters into a competition with Tanneke, at least in her mind, and judges herself to be smarter, better presented and more efficient than the older maid. She quite rightly assumes that Tanneke is threatened by her arrival because she is not actually very good at anything, however her loyalty to the family has stood her in good stead and this is one virtue that Griet does not possess.

Because she feels threatened and sees the unsettling influence that Griet has on the family, Tanneke is quite defensive where Griet is concerned and Griet finds herself using flattery in order to manipulate Tanneke into a good mood.

"The right words changed her mood in a moment."

However, Griet underestimates Tanneke when she assumes she is fickle in her moods and will not stay bad-tempered for long. When Griet really offends her, Tanneke stays mad and ignores Griet even after she leaves the Vermeers. Her basic soft heartedness can be seen however, when she rescues Griet from Van Ruijven, despite being angry with her.

When Griet sees Tanneke again, ten years after Griet's departure from the Vermeer house, the older maid is quite pathetically, still in the same position with no prospect of a better future. She has been badly scarred in a cooking accident and has maintained her bitter grudge against Griet.

Question

Why does Tanneke call Griet a whore after Pieter asks her to marry him?

Minor Characters

Griet's Family

"Working for them has turned your head...It's made you forget who you are and where you come from. We're a decent Protestant family whose needs are not ruled by riches or fashions."

Griet's family are simple working people who rely on each other for financial and emotional support. Her mother is practical, hard working and proud. She refuses charity, makes homemade remedies for her family's ailments and speaks her mind, giving good advice to her daughter when she can see how she has changed. She knows Griet does not always tell her the truth and does not fully trust her but she keeps her advice to herself until she feels it is absolutely necessary.

"She did not speak her mind often. When she did, her words were worth gold."

Griet's father is a shell of a man since his accident. Griet quite correctly tells her brother that her father's apprenticeship in tile making did make him the man he was to become. He is pitied by his neighbours and feels great guilt about his children having to go into service to support him.

"Already you have the scars of hard work."

One of the most tragic things about this book is the growing distance between Griet and her father. Their closeness is evident at the beginning as they discuss paintings and he has obviously passed on his love of art and his sensitivity to colour to his daughter. Griet tries to maintain this common interest with her father after her sister's death and valiantly describes painting after painting in a way that her father can understand. However, as she learns more from Vermeer, she becomes increasingly frustrated with her father's lack of understanding and insistence that there must be a story behind the painting.

Griet notices her father's deterioration after Agnes dies and Frans runs away, describing him as,

"...like a beetle that has fallen onto its back and cannot turn itself over."

Frans is a frustrated and angry young man. Unlike Griet, he is unable to get used to his new life and resents his parents for giving him no choice in his own future. Apart from contact with Griet, he is completely isolated and knows nothing about life outside the monotonous routine of the factory.

With Griet's encouragement he begins visiting home again but his sister notes how obsessed he has become with materialistic things as a result of his abject poverty.

Frans runs away from the factory after a sex scandal that his family is left behind to contend with and is an example of what happens to those who refuse to accept their place in this society.

Agnes is lonely and upset when Griet leaves, having already had to come to terms with her father's blindness and her brother's departure. Griet is haunted by her treatment of Agnes the last time she sees her feeling that she has betrayed her little sister and replaced her with Maertge. Interestingly, it is Maertge that Griet feels the closest to and maintains a relationship with after she leaves the Vermeers, perhaps trying to make up for the way she treated her own little sister.

Question

To what extent are Frans and Griet products of their own upbringing? Use specific examples to support your answer.

Van Leeuwenhoek

Van Leeuwenhoek has a small but significant part to play in the events of the novel. He owns the camera obscura and this item is a major catalyst in the intensifying of the relationship between Griet and Vermeer. Van Leeuwenhoek also serves to confirm some of Griet's opinions for us. He respects Vermeer and is, in fact, Vermeer's only genuine male friend in the novel. It is Van Leeuwenhoek who sees to it that Vermeer's final wishes concerning Griet are carried through.

Van Leeuwenhoek is not very friendly towards Catharina and she fears and avoids him. This also confirms Griet's otherwise biased opinion of Catharina, as Van Leeuwenhoek seems to be a sound judge of character and a respected member of the community of Delft.

Van Leeuwenhoek is a gentleman but he always shows great respect and kindness towards Griet. Griet feels that he pities her when Vermeer treats her with ignorance and he tries to warn her not to get caught in the contest between Vermeer and Van Ruijven.

Griet likes Van Leeuwenhoek and has great respect for his intelligence, his loyalty to her master and his compassion towards her.

Question

What is the most important role Van Leeuwenhoek serves for the purposes of the novel, in your opinion?

THEMATIC CONCERNS

There are many issues raised in this novel. The main thematic concerns you should consider are:

Competition
Sight and Observation
Change
Choices
Place and Power

Competition

"I felt caught between the two men. It was not a pleasant feeling."

Delft is a society based on competition and only those who come out on top survive. Griet herself is a product of this competitive society as evidenced by her appraisal of Tanneke at their first meeting. She notes that Tanneke wore,

"...an apron that was not as clean as mine."

Vermeer must compete against the many other talented painters and artists in the city and his refusal to buy into that contest and sacrifice his art can be seen as a virtue. However, as Van Leeuwenhoek correctly points out to Griet, Vermeer is not averse to entering into a competition with his patron over Griet.

"You see, competition makes men possessive. He is interested in you in part because Van Ruijven is."

Griet is also the prize in the competition between Vermeer and Pieter and although she seems to settle for the butcher, he is in fact a worthy opponent. When he visits Griet's church she notes that a number of girls are competing for Pieter's attention and her parents are willing to let their daughter stand alone in an alley with this handsome young man as they are aware of the fate of poor single women in this society. This prospective husband who is self-sufficient, good-looking, kind and obviously in love with Griet, is also able to feed them and therefore becomes an excellent alternative to their daughter ending up like Tanneke.

Griet's competition with Tanneke seems to be already won in Griet's mind. Initially, she notes everything that the older maid does wrong because Griet does not want to be there. However she comes to feel superior to Tanneke in every way, including the knowledge that she can manipulate Tanneke into a better mood with false flattery, the very vice that Griet hates Van Ruijven for.

Tanneke is right to feel threatened by Griet but she does have one attribute that Griet does not possess, loyalty to the family and Griet will never better her in that regard. Griet often admits to telling Pieter things that she has been specifically asked to keep private by Maria Thins and she has no qualms in desiring and actively pursuing her mistress's husband. Tanneke, in contrast, physically defends Catharina from her violent brother, in spite of the fact that she doesn't really like Catharina very much. Tanneke is especially jealous of the relationship she sees forming between Griet and Maria Thins. She overtly points out "My mistress's rooms" when showing Griet around for the first time and is extremely put out by the fact that Griet is allowed into the studio whenever she pleases. The final straw for Tanneke is when Griet pulls the Maria Thins card using an extremely condescending tone to direct Tanneke to her own mistress for confirmation of Griet's activities. The combination of Griet's rudeness and the knowledge that Maria Thins and Griet share a secret that she does not know about is too much for Tanneke and she cannot forgive the younger maid. Despite Griet's arrogant, "I had won." It is clear that she has also lost something quite valuable, an ally of her own status within the house.

Of course, Griet's main female competition is Catharina whom she sees as an adversary from the outset. Griet often compares herself with her mistress and clearly sees Catharina as incompatible with Vermeer because of her height, her religion and especially her ignorance of the intricacies of his art. When Catharina wants Griet to move back downstairs from the attic, Griet sees it as a challenge to Vermeer to choose between the two women but ultimately she must admit that Vermeer has another mistress that neither Griet nor his own wife can beat. His art takes precedence over anyone or anything and he manipulates both women at various times, using what he needs to complete his paintings to his own satisfaction. In the end they are forced to concede that even in death he controls them.

"..it's not for you to decide. He has decided for you, and for me."

Question

Explore the theme of competition making close reference to character, setting and context within the novel.

Sight and Observation

"Perhaps he does not want to see."

Chevalier relies heavily on her use of the senses to create much of the imagery in the novel. Griet goes into detailed descriptions of how things feel, smell, sound and taste. However none of these senses are as important to the feel of the novel as sight is.

Characters watch each other constantly, either out of suspicion or fascination. In the opening section of the novel the reader becomes aware of Griet's level of scrutiny on others. While Catharina has come to inspect Griet to ascertain whether she will be a suitable maid for her household, it is clear that Catharina herself is under scrutiny from Griet. Her wide eyes are often what get Griet into compromising positions and as Pieter notes, she sees everything but hides her emotional response to what she sees beneath her cap.

Griet's father is blind and his frustration at not being able to see the world around him is accentuated by his insistence that Griet enable him to 'see' the paintings as she does. Her father's eyes have been sown shut since his accident yet he is still able to see the emotional distance that is occurring between his daughter and himself.

When Griet begins working for the Vermeers she feels as if she is under constant scrutiny. Maria Thins watches her to see if she is an efficient worker and often sneaks up behind her to watch her as the story progresses, perhaps pondering how she manages to cause so much trouble. Griet often feels that Vermeer watches her through a window and it is not until he paints her that she realises the emotional distance he watches her from, framing her as if she is in a painting.

Griet is obviously being watched closely by another character, Cornelia, who waits for an opportunity to attack her. In an interesting quote she notes,

"Peeking down at the street below, I spied Tanneke, scrubbing the tiles in front of the house. She did not see me, but a cat padding across the wet tiles behind her paused and looked up."

From then on she closely connects Cornelia with the cat and its sinister presence.

When Vermeer begins to teach Griet about colour and painting, she is enraptured and admits,

"I could not stop looking at things."

She also feels that she has begun to see everyday things with new eyes.

"I had been looking at clouds all my life but I felt as if I saw them for the first time at that moment."

However, Griet finds it difficult to separate what she sees in a painting from reality. When she first sees Van Ruijven's wife she cannot take her eyes off her as she is so used to seeing her in the painting, but she also notes that studying something beautiful too closely, detracts from its beauty and this becomes true in her image of who Vermeer really is.

One of the reason Griet feels that Catharina is incompatible with Vermeer is her inability to understand his work. When she asks Catharina if she should clean the windows in the studio and explains the effect of the lighting on the painting, Catharina, "did not see." Catharina avoids studying her husband's paintings too closely also; obviously afraid to enter the studio and intimidated by what she does not comprehend. Her carelessness with the camera obscura and her subsequent fear of Van Leeuwenhoek (a man who sees things very clearly as they are) represent her inability to see as Griet and Vermeer do. In contrast, she sees Griet very clearly for what she is; a young woman who desires her belongings, her husband and her position as mistress of the house.

The camera obscura becomes the biggest symbol for seeing in the novel. Vermeer uses the tool so that he can see better, explaining to Griet,

"My eyes do not always see everything."

While Vermeer has excellent vision for seeing what is needed in his paintings, he is blind to real life and chooses not to see the effect he is having on those around him, especially Griet. He is ignorant of her situation and turns away when she really needs him to see her. Ultimately Griet is forced to admit that he only sees people as possible subjects for his art and cannot see beyond that.

Question

Van Ruijven tells Griet that Vermeer "sees the world as he wants it to be, not as it is." What is the difference between what Vermeer sees and what is real?

Change

"It all felt strange, this sudden movement and change after weeks of stillness and quiet."

Griet is a character who is extremely resistant to change. This is understandable considering the transitions she has been forced to make and the upheavals in her life before and during the time period of the novel.
She has had to deal with firstly her father's accident and along with this a complete change in lifestyle and status for her family. She ponders the effect on herself and her two siblings, often reminiscing about their carefree childhood and considering how Frans has changed as a result of having to leave home and how Agnes will have to

grow up more quickly because of her own departure form home. She explains her fear of change when she compares Aleydis to herself.

"She had looked after her sisters as I had looked after my brother and sister. That made a girl cautious and wary of change."

The canal becomes a symbol for Griet, partly because it reminds her of her brother and sister before all the changes took place but also because water itself is a symbol of change as it moves and alters things, changes its form from liquid to ice and becomes stagnant and stale if it stays still too long. As much as Griet resists the changes that happen, she is forced to accommodate them and ultimately, is much happier when she accepts them and moves on with her life.

Griet constantly compares her old life to her new one when she first moves to the Vermeer's. Her 'pie slices' have been ruined and nothing satisfies her in her new home as it is strange and different. She finds fault with everything and everyone until she finds a familiar place in Vermeer's studio. Her father is correct when he notes that this is the only part of her new life that she initially likes and it is partly because it reminds her of her father that she feels comfortable there. Like Vermeer, she sees it as an escape, but for her, it is an escape from all the changes she has had to deal with.

Another reason she is comfortable in the studio is that nothing seems to change very much. She can do the same thing every day and it comforts her to see the predictability and stillness of the room and the painting setting. If Vermeer changes something in the scene or the painting, she notices immediately and in her mind their relationship builds in this way.

Top Notes

However, Griet also starts to obsess about changes that Vermeer makes. If she cannot predict what he is going to do she is disturbed by it; "The change upset me."

Griet shows a real development in her identity when in a bold move she dares to make a change to Vermeer's setting. The move unsettles her as it is uncharacteristic but she is thrilled to discover that Vermeer, "made my change." And from then on she seems more prepared to face the changes that she knows will inevitably happen in her life.

In fact, when the time comes for her to leave the Vermeers, she makes the decision herself, turning and leaving before anyone can tell her to go.

Question

List the changes that Griet must deal with throughout the course of the novel. How does she deal with each of them?

Choices

"I have no choice I'm afraid."

Chevalier stresses the limited choices available to women in this society. Griet has no choice in whether she goes to work for the Vermeers or not, she must help support her family. She has little choice over whom she marries and her reluctance to marry Pieter when she clearly does have feelings for him has more to do with her exercising a little control over her own life than it does with him. Griet also often refers to the things Vermeer asks her to do as compulsory.

"But he was my master. I was meant to do as he said."

Tanneke is another character with no choice in the life she must lead. Her status and personage ensure that the only life she can hope for is one of servitude. This is part of the reason she is so angry with Griet after Pieter proposes to her. Griet's beauty and superior mind clearly give her marginally more choice than Tanneke will ever have, and the life of boring servitude that Griet sees stretching before her is actually a reality for the older maid. However, Catharina, despite her superior status, evidently has very little control over her own life either. Tanneke's insistence that Catharina is filling the house with children because she cannot fill it with servants is a little unfair given the knowledge that Catharina cannot actually refuse her husband if he wants her. According to Griet, Catharina really does not enjoy being pregnant. She is uncomfortable and cumbersome and it is perhaps not her choice to be that way. She also has no control over her husband's comings and goings or how quickly he paints. When she gives him a choice between the jewellery box and Griet, he ignores both of her options, coming up with his own solution to the problem. Catharina makes it very clear to Griet by the end of the novel that neither of them had choices where Vermeer was concerned.

"He has decided for you and for me."

Frans is frustrated and angry at the life he is forced to lead and makes the choice to escape but Griet feels she cannot follow this path. It is unthinkable that she should leave her parents hungry when she has the opportunity to ensure they eat meat every day. Interestingly, for someone who has insisted she had no choice throughout the novel, she lists a number of options she could take by the end of the novel but the reader knows ultimately which one she will take. It is the only viable one for everyone involved. She marries Pieter.

Question

"In our favourite game, one of us chose a point and one of us named a thing – a stork, a church, a wheelbarrow, a flower – and we ran in that direction looking for that thing."

What is Griet looking for when she makes her final choice?

Place and Power

"He set a chair near his easel facing the middle window and I sat down. I knew it was to be my place."

Chevalier intends the reader to closely examine the concept of placement, displacement and replacement as well as considering the effects of various physical places on characters within the text.

'Place' is an interesting concept. It can mean a person's position in life as well as a physical area. While the city of Delft provides the artistic backdrop for the novel, it is the place that Griet finds herself in when she is 'placed' at the Vermeer's that is worth exploring.

Griet is very aware of her place in life and can see the divisions in her society. However she is not pleased with her status, often comparing herself favourably with those she feels do not deserve their place, especially Catharina. Once employed by the Vermeers, Griet is more aware than ever of her place in life. Catharina calls her 'nothing' and the apothecary does not remember her despite seeing her the previous afternoon because she is part of the invisible serving class.

However, Griet admits to finding her place in her new situation and eventually finds herself replacing her old life with her new one.

"I was beginning to forget where my mother kept things...After only a few months I could describe the house in Papists Corner better than my family's."

This results in tragic consequences, as she is unable to ease the guilt of the last time she sees Agnes is when her sister is staring at her 'replacement', Maertge.
Her position or place is a precarious one and this is made clear when she is concerned about losing her place if Vermeer does not paint faster. Frans is in a similar position when he nearly loses his place due to his inappropriate behaviour. Griet warns him, hypocritically,

"Frans, you know she's not for the likes of you. To endanger your place here for something like that."

There are a number of characters that abuse the power that their place in life affords. Van Ruijven pursues young women who have little choice to refuse him with no thought for where they may end up as a result of his attention. Catharina abuses her servants, showing them no respect and knowing that no one will check her behaviour and Vermeer places an ever increasing work load on Griet with no thought of how she will complete it and keep his secret. However, Griet will not blame him for anything symbolically resuming her place when he complains that she has moved position.
"Griet's great attribute in the studio is that she is good at exactly replacing items where they were after she has cleaned them and that she can instinctively feel when something is out of place. Her disquiet at her own positional changes as she develops emotionally, mentally

and sexually are reflected in her sensitivity to the importance of the placement of objects within the paintings.

Question

Griet goes through a number of place changes in the novel. Who is most effective in putting her in the appropriate place?

LANGUAGE ANALYSIS

Chevalier's use of language is one of the reasons her books are so successful. Her dense description and clever depiction of images contribute to the rich atmosphere and intense emotion of the story. You should identify specific language techniques and explain their effect on you as a reader and responder to this text.

The most obvious language technique used is first person narrative. The whole story is told from the perspective of Griet and the reader is therefore heavily influenced by Griet's feelings about other characters. However, Chevalier has cleverly allowed the reader further insight into other characters through other language devices. Chevalier often utilises similes to get an image or feeling across to the reader.

"Agnes had a hoarse voice as if her throat were covered with cobwebs."

"She moved down the hallway like a ship with its sails full."

"I felt like an apple tree losing its fruit."

Often her comparisons are ambiguous in meaning and use animals and birds to create a sense of the person's character. Vermeer's interest in Griet becomes predatory as he tests her intelligence.

"His face became intent like a stork's when it sees a fish it can catch."

Catharina is praised and criticised when Griet compares her to a swan.

"Catharina remained in bed...serene as a swan. Like a swan too, she had a long neck and a sharp beak."

The ideas presented often have greater connotations, linking cleverly to the images already woven into the narrative in an intricate pattern.

"Hearing his voice made me feel as if I were walking along the edge of a canal and unsure of my steps."

Griet has previously related the story of the game she would play with her siblings, dropping stones in the murky depths of the canal, imagining the monsters that lurked at the bottom. This description shows that while she likes and feels connected to the canal, just as she likes and respects Vermeer, she is also afraid and mystified by its secrets and she is also frightened of what lies at the mysterious depths of this man.

Chevalier also employs metaphors and symbolism to great effect in the novel. The metaphor of light is particularly relevant, as Vermeer was known as the artist of light. His specialty was his ability to use light to reflect colour rather than seeing colour as intrinsic to the artwork. Chevalier often refers to Griet's sensitivity to the light and her comprehension of how important it was to Vermeer's art is the main reason their relationship develops. Griet refers to being enlightened by Vermeer and the degree of light in the studio is a good reflection of how Griet is feeling.

"He had opened all the shutters. I had never seen the room so bright."

Apart from the figurative imagery she uses, Chevalier also uses concrete imagery and small details create vivid images.

"Instead we watched the boats go up and down the canal, full on their way to market with cabbages, pigs, flowers, wood, flour, strawberries, horseshoes. They were empty on their way back, the boatmen counting money or drinking. I taught the girls games I had played with Agnes and Frans, and they taught me games they had made up. They blew bubbles, played with their dolls, ran with their hoops, while I sat on the bench with Johannes in my lap."

This small passage is loaded with detail that depicts daily life on the canal as well as the growing relationship between Griet and the Vermeer children.

Contrast is a simple language tool that Chevalier uses to both set up conflict situations and provide a clear sense of how the narrator feels about various situations and characters. Griet often compares herself to other characters, especially Tanneke and Catharina. She also sets the Vermeer's home up against her family home and items such as her grandmother's tortoiseshell comb against Catharina's. When Griet describes and condones the baker's simple but genuine approval of the painting of his daughter, Griet effectively condemns Van Ruijven's false praise at the same time.

One of the biggest juxtapositions is between the two men in Griet's life. Pieter and Vermeer are constantly compared, the most dominant image being their hands. While Griet is bothered by Pieter's blood stained hands, she sees Vermeer's hands as being very clean.

One of the most important language devices used is symbolism. There are many symbols created by Chevalier and already existing in the artwork of Vermeer that she chooses to use. The symbol represents something else by association, resemblance or convention. For example, Griet refers to the painting process that Vermeer uses and describes the paintings as 'growing'. This whole process could be an elaborate symbol for the relationship that Griet sees growing between herself and the painter.

"There were areas of colour that did not make things."

Explain the symbolic meaning of the following. Consider what greater meaning they could have and how they can make you understand characters and themes better.

- The vegetable wheel
- Catharina's keys
- Linseed oil
- The cat
- Griet's hair
- The tile
- The canal
- Light
- The window
- The hanging
- The colours
- The earring

Because the genre of this novel is historical fiction, Chevalier has used many factual historical features to create realism and a sense of atmosphere in the novel. She has studied the paintings she has used carefully then used considerable poetic license to create an imaginary story behind the making of each. Details of Vermeer's real life and the real people who he associated with are also used.

The language of *Girl with a Pearl Earring* is extremely dense and no words are wasted. You should practise analysing segments of language, looking carefully at the passage's significance to the ideas of the novel as a whole and using language features such as the ones suggested above to write a sophisticated and articulate answer.

MODEL ESSAY

Read carefully the question below and then examine the essay outline on the following pages. Try to develop your essay along these lines and develop strategies to answer questions.

The VCE English written examination in 2003 asked students to answer two essays. The first essay in the text response section required students to: 'develop a sustained interpretive point of view about a text, supported by detailed analysis and reference to the text.

The second essay required ' a developed and sustained discussion that analyses the underlying social or cultural values embodied in a text.

Remember that you MUST write on different texts in parts one and two.

QUESTION

'But what is the story in the painting?'
'His paintings don't tell stories.' "
What does Tracy Chevalier's story tell us about 17th Century Delft and the societal constraints placed on its inhabitants?

This question is asking you to identify societal constraints on the individual in 17th Century Delft. You should choose one character and examine the restraints placed on that individual throughout the novel, considering how the character responds to these restrictions. You could also compare another character to consider the contrast between people in this society from different walks of life. As this is basically a context question, your knowledge of Delft in Vermeer's time will greatly inform your response. However, the novel itself is your first reference point and Chevalier has included a wealth of information regarding societal restraints on her characters, most notably on her female characters.

Griet is from a poor working class Protestant family. Her father's accident has further impoverished them but their pride does not allow them to take public charity so Griet is forced to take on a maid's position in a Catholic household. Already you have a number of conflicts to deal with.

Other characters are forced to contend with the restraints placed on them by their financial status, religion or class. Even the Vermeers are at the mercy of their wealthy patron and must fall in with his wishes in order to survive financially. But it is Griet's family who is most dependent on their daughter making a good match. If she chooses not to marry Pieter, what would happen to her family? Her brother has already neglected his responsibility, Griet has little choice but to do the right thing, even though she resents the deal being made over her head and feels like a piece of meat.

You could also compare Griet's position as a female in this society with Tanneke, Catharina and Maria Thins. This is a society where women are treated as sexual objects or commodities to be traded. Catharina's position is marginally more secure than Griet's and on a number of occasions, Griet must reject sexual advances and suggestive comments from men who see her as fair game. Consider the boatman and the soldiers as well as Van Ruijven.

It would be a good idea to choose some of the paintings Chevalier has used and integrate them into your argument. There is no need to discuss their artistic worth, but the author has used them as a way of interpreting issues in this society. Consider especially the title piece and *The Girl with the Wineglass.* Both texts show a vulnerable female looking out of the picture. What does this world offer these women?

Other issues prevalent in this society include the nature of competition and debt. What is it about this society that has created an atmosphere of contest and a sense that everyone owes somebody something. Griet cannot take favours from anyone without feeling like she is indebted to them. Indeed her reaction to receiving the pearl earrings at the end of the novel is to repay the debt she feels she owes her husband.

"A maid came free."

Even though the question mentions the story behind the paintings, do not fall into the trap of retelling the story. The story involves several aspects: theme, setting, character and context. You should discuss these using language features and discussing the paintings contextually. Always refer back to the quote and question taking special care to integrate quotes as evidence to back up your sustained logical argument.

THE ESSAY

The essay has been the subject of numerous texts and you should have the basic form well in hand. As teachers, the point we would emphasise would be to link the paragraphs both to each other and back to your argument (which should directly respond to the question). Of course ensure your argument is logical and sustained.

Make sure you use specific examples and that your quotes are accurate. To ensure that you respond to the question make sure you plan carefully and are sure what relevant point each paragraph is making. It is solid technique to actually 'tie up' each point by explicitly coming back to the question.

When composing an essay the basic conventions of the form are:

- State your argument, outline the points to be addressed and perhaps have a brief definition.

↓

A solid structure for each paragraph is:
- Topic sentence *(the main idea and its link to the previous paragraph/argument)*
- Explanation / discussion of the point including links between texts if applicable.
- Detailed evidence *(Close textual reference- quotes, incidents and technique discussion.)*
- Tie up by restating the point's relevance to argument / question

↓

- Summary of points
- Final sentence that restates your argument

As well as this basic structure you will need to focus on:

Audience – for the essay the audience must be considered formal unless specifically stated otherwise. Therefore your language must reflect the audience. This gives you the opportunity to use the jargon and vocabulary that you have learnt in English. For the audience ensure your introduction is clear and has impact. Avoid slang or colloquial language including contractions (like doesn't, eg., etc.).

Purpose – the purpose of the essay is to answer the question given. The examiner evaluates how well you can make an argument and understand the issues and its text(s). An essay is solidly structured so its composer can analyse ideas. This is where you earn marks. It does not retell the story or state the obvious.

Communication – Take a few minutes to plan the essay. If you rush into your answer it is almost certain you will not make the most of the brief 40 minutes to show all you know about the question. More likely you will include irrelevant details that do not gain you marks but waste your precious time.

Remember an essay is formal so **do not** do the following: story-tell, list and number points, misquote, use slang or colloquial language, be vague, use non sentences or fail to address the question.

MODEL ESSAY – *Girl with a Pearl Earring*

Question: Why is Tracy Chevalier's portrayal of the concept of 'Place' in the novel *Girl with a Pearl Earring* so significant to the overall concerns of the novel?

A few notes about the question:

- Remember the actual question is asking you what you have learned about the importance of *Girl with a Pearl Earring*

- The quote that begins the question is more to point you in the right direction.

- It is important you take note of the ideas the quote raises and check your response does address them.

- Take care that you write on different texts in the two sections.

- You MUST have quotations and textual references that show you have a good knowledge and understanding of your text.

- Your response must remember to focus on what that part is specifically examining. You can do this by answering the question carefully.

ESSAY RESPONSE

Question: Why is Tracy Chevalier's portrayal of the concept of 'Place' in the novel *Girl with a Pearl Earring* so significant to the overall concerns of the novel?

There are obvious reasons why Tracy Chevalier has paid so much attention to the portrayal of place in the novel *Girl with a Pearl Earring*. The novel takes its name from the painting by Johannes Vermeer, which was painted in Delft in the 17th Century so it is necessary that the reader understand the setting that the work was created in. However, the place of Delft with its art history and Renaissance conflicts is only one aspect of the place puzzle that exists in this novel. The author also intends the reader to closely examine the concept of placement, displacement and replacement in life and examines the extent to which society dictates an individual's place.

The vivid descriptions of Delft as the background setting for the story of Griet and her experiences with the Vermeer family evoke a powerful portrayal of place. The setting is important because Delft was a centre of artistic creation and the home of the real Johannes Vermeer. The society of Delft is a rigid one – there are accepted class and religious divisions and the inhabitants of Delft know the consequences of stepping out of their place.

Griet herself is very aware of her 'place' or status in society but does not necessarily accept this place. She wears her cap in such a way as to hide her true feelings from the world but beneath her calm exterior, experiences a range of emotional reactions to the world she lives in. When we first meet Griet, she is chopping vegetables, carefully 'placing' them in their correct colour scheme on the vegetable wheel. When she hears the voices of the Vermeers speaking to her mother in the next room, she is quick to recognise the money and status in their voices.

"I could hear rich carpets in their voices, books and pearls and fur."

In contrast, Griet's mother sounds to her like, "a cooking pot, a flagon."
The distinction between the privileged and the working class is clearly made.
When Griet sees the strangers for the first time she notices their heights, immediately judging the taller woman to be incompatible with her husband. Griet also notes that her own family, including her father and brother, is small. The inference made is that this smallness applies to their status as well as their stature. Griet is given a placement at the Vermeers, further emphasising her lowly status as part of the serving class. She feels displaced, critical of all the differences she sees and comparing everything to what she knows as familiar. When she returns home on the first Sunday, she finds herself close to tears as she relaxes into familiarity.

"I felt my back relaxing into the pew and my face softening from the mask I had worn all week."

It does not take long however, for Griet to feel more settled in her new home.

"I began to find my place at the house on the Oude Langendijk."

In fact, the displacement she originally felt becomes replacement as Griet is unable to come to terms with the two worlds she is a part of and gradually feels one usurping the other. Her mother notices this in Griet, observing that,

"Working for them has turned your head...It's made you forget who you are and where you come from. We're a decent Protestant family whose needs are not ruled by riches or fashions."

Pieter the butcher also puts Griet in her place when she is rude to him reminding her the she had, "..best get used to flies." But by far the most effective at telling Griet her proper place is Catharina who informs Van Ruijven that Griet is "only the maid" and later that she is "nothing."

Griet is often afraid of losing her place and is careful to do the best job she can. Maria Thins reminds her that her place is not so secure and Griet feels she must help Vermeer to paint faster in order to retain her position. Griet's perfectionist nature is ideal for her main job which is to carefully clean Vermeer's studio, replacing the items in his setting after cleaning them, so that the scene appears to have not been disturbed.

"This is how I cleaned without seeming to move anything. I measured each thing in relation to the objects around it and the space between them."

This is also the way Griet judges people. Measuring each person carefully based on who is around them and the space between them. Ironically she misjudges the space between Vermeer and herself, believing them to be closer than they are and forgetting the emotional barrier he places between himself and others. She forgets also her own status and the importance of not disturbing the social order. Although she clearly understands the danger of displacing even one object in the painting setting, she forgets that this reflects the society she lives in. When she looks to Maria Thins and Vermeer to defend her, she realises that ultimately they agree with Catharina's summation that Griet is 'nothing'.

Griet is left to find her true place with the only real alternative left for her. While she has compared the Meat Market's blood stains and tang of blood in the air unfavourably with the sterile environment of Vermeer's studio, she must finally accept that this is the direction her life must take and she finds her place as the butcher predicted with Pieter.

Griet's experience reflects a universal one of individuals trying to find their place in life despite societal expectations and restraints. Ultimately, despite her belief that the system is unfair and some people do not deserve the place they have, Griet is forced to admit that she cannot deny who she is. Her confusion about her identity gradually dissipates as she finds her place with her new husband and new life. Not a maid and not a lady, "Just Griet."

GLOSSARY

Apothecary	Equivalent of a Chemist
Canal	Artificial waterway
Camera obscura	Ancestor of the photographic camera. Latin translation means Dark chamber
Catholicism	The adherence to belief of true church being led by direct line of bishops from Peter.
Calvinism	Followers of John Calvin who led Protestant Reformation in France, emphasising predestination and adherence to strict moral code in 16th Century Europe.
Ermine	Fur of a weasel like creature
Flagon	Large bottle
Guild	Organisation of persons with common business interests formed for mutual aid or protection
Guilders	Dutch currency
Lapis Lazuli	Deep blue stone
Linseed oil	Oil maid from flax
Mantle	Cloak or coat
Mary Magdalene	Prostitute who became a follower of Christ in the New Testament
New Church	Dutch Reformed Protestant Church

Papists	Followers of the Pope i.e. Catholics
Paternity Cap	Hat worn by new fathers in celebration of the birth of their new child
Portrait	Painting of a single figure
Protestants	Followers of the new church formed after The Reformation led by John Calvin.
Quarantine	Strict isolation designed to prevent the spread of disease.
Plague	The epidemic disease of high mortality that killed thousands of people in Europe during the 17th Century
Still Life	Painting of objects such as a fruit bowl or group of ornaments
Stuivers	Dutch currency
Schie River	River in Delft
Rotterdam	City in Holland
Tortoise shell	Hard mottled substance used to make luxury items such as decorative combs
Ochre	Pigment ranging in colour from yellow to orange-brown
Vermilion	Brilliant scarlet red
Madder	Maroon or ruby red
William Of Orange	Protestant
Palette	Wooden slate to mix colours on used by artists.